Football's Multiple Pro-I Offense

RON COSNER

PARKER PUBLISHING COMPANY, INC.

West Nyack, NY

Library of Congress Cataloging in Publication Data

Cosner, Ron,
    Football's multiple pro-I offense.

    Includes index.
    1. Football—Offense. 2. Football coaching.
I. Title.
GV951.8.C67   796.33'22   78-25850
ISBN 0-13-324137-8

Printed in the United States of America

Dedication

*To my wife Shaaron, "Rab" Currie, my high
school coach in Charleroi, Pennsylvania,
Frank Kush at Arizona State University, and
to all Padre Football players, past, present,
and future.*

WHAT THIS BOOK
OFFERS YOU

Football's Multiple Pro-I Offense explains how to combine the separate elements of a simple offense for more scoring punch. These pages describe an offense that is easily communicated and demonstrated to players, an especially important factor in pre-college football where practice time is short and you, the coach, must work with the given personnel since you cannot recruit. By employing the Pro-I Multiple Offense, you will see how to eliminate mistakes, make time for perfecting the basics, and incorporate just enough plays to cover a given situation yet keep them so simple that confusion is eliminated even under stress.

In addition to the basic terminology and sets necessary for initiating the Pro-I, this book offers ways of identifying personnel characteristics and special skills needed for placing the player in the position that is best for him and best for the offense. Hints on proper stance and spacing and basic blocking rules set the stage for introducing the Pro-I.

The offense includes techniques of initiating the running game, inside and out, along with the dives, counters, slants, and slips of the former and the options and sweeps for the latter. A successful trapping game plan with routes and blocking is included, while roll out and drop back passing techniques round out the passing game you will need to balance the offensive attack.

Play action pass blocking rules in the Pro-I help teach techniques needed for a successful passing attack off the running game. A "passing tree" is included to capitalize on the pass routes and drills—including those helpful to linemen, such as the sweeps, trap and pass blocking, and play action—and to help you improve the skills of the various positions. These drills will give you a solid base from which to develop an offensive line while the receiver drills—crack back blocking, blocking downfield, release drills from the line of scrimmage, and pattern running—help to improve receiver skills. The back drills—looking for the holes and blocking and passing routes—enable you to improve backfield skills while the quarterback drills stress the responsibility of that position for running and passing plays. Incorporated within all these chapters are the basics needed to attack some of the more common defenses your team might come up against.

By following the techniques illustrated in this book and putting the simple components together, you will achieve a solid base from which to start. Later you can add your own ideas and techniques as you get used to the offense and your knowledge of the various defenses used against it increases. You can be sure that this offense will never stagnate, and it can be easily changed to meet the challenges of each season—of each new team.

Ron Cosner

Acknowledgments

I would like to acknowledge and thank my assistant coaches, Mike Crowe, Bob Urchike, and Tom Huber for their help during the preparation of this book.

CONTENTS

11

1

HOW TO CAPITALIZE
ON THE PRO-I OFFENSE

Darrell Royal, former coach of the University of Texas, once called the basics of football the flour and salt and meal of the game and said, ". . .if you try to mix them with a lot of other fancy ingredients you may miss out on your daily bread."[1] This, in a nutshell, is the philosophy behind the success enjoyed by the Pro-I offense—simplicity—the art of moving the football, maintaining possession, getting that first down, and scoring points without the use of "fancy ingredients" to cause confusion.

In keeping with the simplicity of the Pro-I, the terms and formation necessary for a basic understanding of the offense are

---

[1]From the book *Darrell Royal Talks Football* by Darrell Royal © 1963 by Prentice-Hall, Inc. Published by Prentice-Hall, Inc., Eaglewood Cliffs, New Jersey.

discussed in the following section. Many of the terms are shortened or abbreviated to sustain even further simplicity and encourage better communications between players and coach. The formations used consist mainly of variations of one basic set. By changing this one set subtly, the offense is given a different look while basically running the same plays.

TERMINOLOGY

B.A.S. (Block Area Solid): BAS is used to describe the offensive lineman blocking the most dangerous man in the area, usually the man on. This term includes the offensive lineman's assignments adjacent to cross blocks, some traps, and the basic three block *(Diagram 1–1)*.

B.I.B. (Block Inside Backer): BIB is a rule in which the offensive lineman blocks the first linebacker to his inside. Blocking a linebacker is one of the most difficult tasks for an offensive lineman. The BIB block simplifies this task by creating an angle which clears the running lane of the linebacker *(Diagram 1–2)*.

Diagram 1–1   *Diagram 1–2*

Crack Back Block: The wide receivers block back to the inside on a defensive end or linebacker on or near the line of scrimmage in the crack back block. It is used on wide running plays and must be made above the waist with the head in front of the defender in accord with recent rule changes.

Cut Block: The cut block is made by an offensive lineman

throwing his head and shoulders at the feet of the defensive lineman, cutting them out from underneath him. This block is used for the quick passing game and some running plays in which offensive linemen must block a defensive lineman toward the hole.

Fold Block: The fold block is a variation of the trap block in which the guard comes around the center (folds) and attacks the linebacker head on. It is used to give the linebacker a different look at the trapping game and is good if the opposing linebacker is particularly tough, as he can be double teamed by combining the trap man with the fold block and the BIB blocker.

G.O.B. (Guards Opposite Backs): The GOB is a passing play in which the backs go in one direction and the guards pull in another. It is used when the defense rotates quickly with the offensive backfield flow. Because it brings back the receiver against the grain, making it difficult for the defense to cover, it is a great play action pass. The guards will always go opposite the backfield flow called in the huddle, their job being to protect the quarterback and lead him upfield if necessary.

I.O.B. (Inside Out Block): The IOB, another way of describing the trap block route to be discussed in Chapter 6, employs the trapper with an inside out angle on the defensive lineman to be trapped.

J-Block: The J-block is executed by the running backs blocking the defensive ends and is used by lead backs in running plays designed to go off tackle. If correctly run, the route should form the shape of the letter "J."

Lead Block: The lead block is the second part of the double team. The offensive lineman will block down on the defensive lineman at his hip, sealing off the running lane. The lead and post blocks are used on trapping plays and some offensive tackle plays *(Diagram 1–3).*

Diagram 1-3   *Diagram 1-4*

M.O.M.A. *(Man on; Man Away):* MOMA is a term used mostly in the trapping game, although it could be used in any running game where the center is to block away from the hole. Usually a center rule, "man on" means the down lineman nose on. "Man away" means the down lineman away from the hole *(Diagram 1-4)*.

Post Block: The post block consists of the man head on with the defensive lineman to be double teamed. The main job is to cut off penetration *(Diagram 1-5)*.

Round Off: The round off is a blocking route taken by the lead backs through the hole on certain running plays. It is often used on an off tackle play, and is negotiated by leading the

Diagram 1-5

ball carrier through the hole and looking to block anyone to his inside, usually the linebacker *(Diagram 5-18)*.

Seam Block: A seam block is a technique whereby the linemen block the inside seam toward the direction of the flow, which in turn is determined in the huddle. The tackle on the side of the call is the pivot point. All linemen must protect the inside seam (toward that tackle) on this pass block.

Screen Block: In the screen block, the offensive lineman puts his body between the defensive lineman and the ball carrier, usually in a stand-up position. (It is not necessary to knock

the defensive man down or drive him back with this block.)
The screen block is good on quick hitting plays where a
small running lane is needed.

S.U.B.A. *(Set Up Block Away):* The SUBA is used to influence the defensive lineman to his outside on the trap play by
attacking his outside shoulder and drawing him away from
the center of the line. The SUBA is not an aggressive block,
for the defensive man who is being "SUBAed" on will be
trapped. After contact is made, the offensive lineman will
turn his back and block the first man to the outside of the
SUBA man *(Diagram 1–6).*

Diagram 1–6

Formations

Basic I: Ninety percent of our offense is run from the Basic I.
We use it because we can hit quickly to all areas due to the
positioning of the two running backs. The only disadvantage to this offense is the lack of the quick pitch play to the
outside *(Diagram 1–7).*

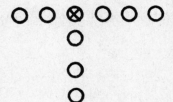

Diagram 1–7 *I Formation*

Brown Formation; Gold Formation; White Formation: These
formations are variations of the Basic I. Some plays must

have the halfback instead of an I, such as the back tackle trap in our offense. In this case, with these variations, the quick pitch can be added to either side and can be run depending on which formation is called. The regular split-T can also be run with these formations. Only one or two plays of our regular offense would be eliminated. All roll out passes, drop back passes, and most play action passes can be run without any loss of effect. Ninety percent of these three formations represent ninety percent of our offense, giving the defense a different look. For example, with a fullback dive right or left, the plays could be run from the I, brown, gold, or white formation *(Diagrams 1–8, 1–9, & 1–10)*.

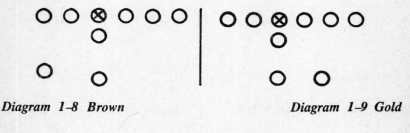

Diagram 1–8 Brown   *Diagram 1–9 Gold*

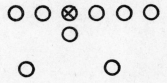

Diagram 1–10 White

Slot: The slot formation is used to give a double receiver a look from one side to the other and can be used for an extra blocker to the slot side. The running backs can use any of the sets as the play is designed to go with the slot formation—for example, brown slot, gold slot, white slot, and so on *(Diagram 1–11)*.

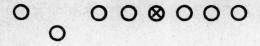

Diagram 1–11 **Slot**

    Strong Right and Left: The strong right and left is used on short yardage plays or when a team has three big backs and likes to grind out yardage. Our freshman team finds this formation extremely effective because of the extra running back and/or blocker. Pop Warner teams might find it effective for the same reason. All of our offense theoretically could be run from this offensive set, the biggest disadvantage being that one wide receiver is lost *(Diagrams 1–12 & 1–13)*.

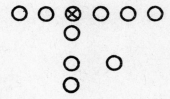

Diagram 1–12 Power-right

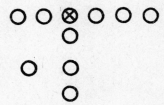

Diagram 1–13 Power-left

    Tight End Left: The tight end left formation is used to get two receivers to the left side. It also changes the defensive strong side and may cause some confusion if the whole defense adjusts to your strong side. The whole offense may be used with this particular formation *(Diagram 1–14)*.

○ ○ ○ ⊗ ○ ○   ○

Diagram 1–14   **Tight End Left**

Any combination of these basic formations can be used, giving the defense a different offensive set. Examples of combining two basic formations may be seen in *Diagrams 1–15, 1–16, & 1–17.*

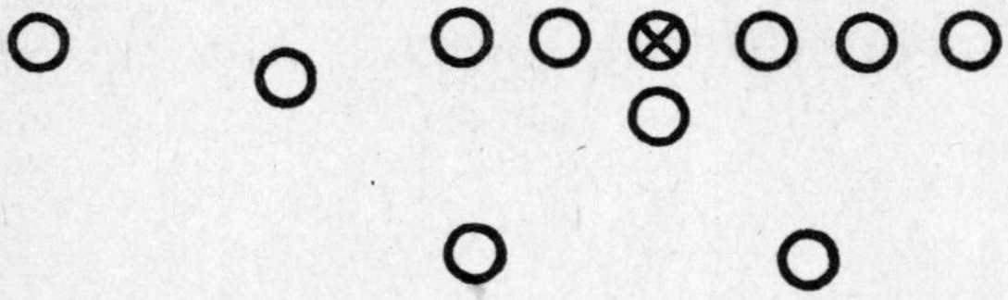

○   ○   ○ ○ ⊗ ○ ○ ○
                 ○
            ○   ○

Diagram 1–15   **White Slot**

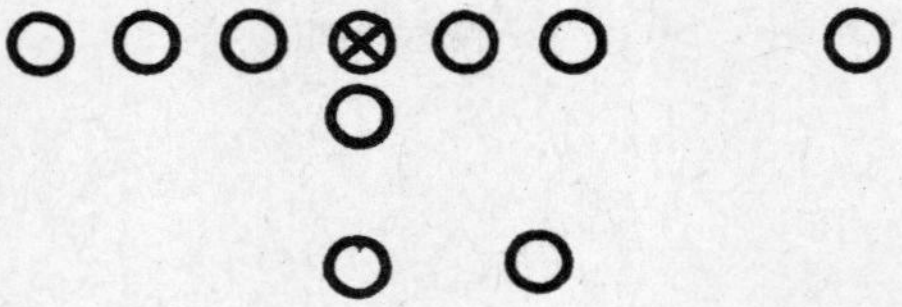

○ ○ ○ ⊗ ○ ○   ○
        ○
      ○   ○

Diagram 1–16   **Tight Left Gold**

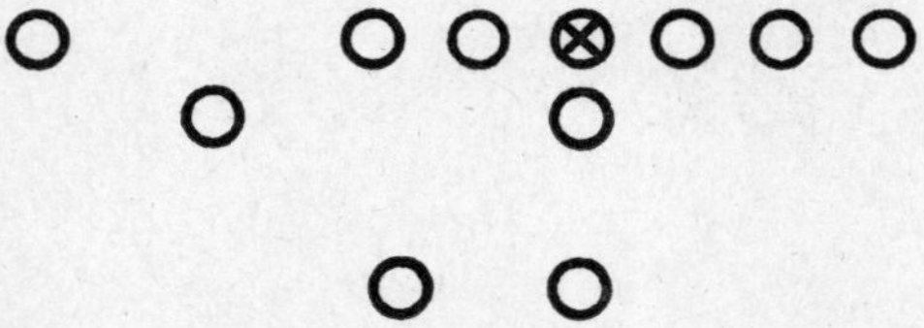

○   ○ ○ ⊗ ○ ○ ○
   ○   ○
      ○   ○

Diagram 1–17   **Brown Slot**

2

IDENTIFYING
A WINNING PRO-I

When our coaching staff sits down to evaluate personnel returning from last year's squad, along with youngsters coming up from the junior varsity or freshman teams, we try to place them in a position that will suit their natural ability even though this may be contrary to the position they nave been playing throughout their sports careers. The positioning in the Multiple Pro-I offense is so simple that if a boy is changed to a different position on varsity he will have little trouble making the adjustment. We have sometimes had to change the positions, for instance, of some of the larger boys.

Many coaches have a tendency to play the bigger boys at running back because they are able to run over the smaller players. In high school this same youngster would not necessarily play at running back. We look at the overall picture—his speed, agility, and backfield common sense—and determine where he will help us most when he reaches the varsity level. Because of this, this particular player might end up playing the line if we felt this was his natural position; and using the Pro-I he would have little trouble making the adjustment to his new position.

In addition, no position is so demanding in this offense that it will drain a player, physically or mentally, regardless of his experience. With the premise in mind then, that most players may be easily rotated to a different position, the general characteristics that the coach should consider when selecting and placing personnel for positions in the Multiple Pro-I offense are listed below.

PRO-I INTERIOR LINEMEN

The Weakside Tackle. The weakside tackle in the Multiple Pro-I offense could be the smallest of the two tackles because there is not as much one-on-one blocking on his side as there is on the strong side. The tackles on this side have averaged between 165 and 175 pounds over the last three years on our squads. We have had one All-Conference player, for instance, who weighed in at 170 pounds. The weakside tackle should possess enough speed to pull to either side; so quickness is this player's biggest asset. He is also agile enough and strong enough to control his area by using different blocking combinations so that he does not have to block one on one more than necessary. The weakside running game in this offense will depend greatly on the ability of the weakside tackle to use his agility, quickness and blocking combinations to the best advantage.

The Strongside Tackle. The strongside tackle, inversely, should be the strongest and biggest lineman because most plays are run at him (and the strongside guard), and most blocks are straight on or within one man on either side of him with hardly any pulling involved. He must be hard-nosed for the same reason—and also because he will be facing the defensive tackle, usually the biggest lineman on the defensive line. Our strongside tackles have averaged between 190 and 200 pounds. We look for height at this position, although it is not absolutely necessary.

The Weakside Guard. The weakside guard in the Pro-I possesses the same general characteristics as the weakside tackle, except that he may be smaller because he has less one-on-one blocking to worry about. He is able to pull on sweeps either way; and, as with the weakside tackle, his biggest asset is quickness. He is able to trap, although he will not be doing as much trapping as the strongside guard. As with the case of the weakside tackle, quickness, agility and use of blocking combinations will greatly enhance the ability of a weakside attack. Our weakside guards have ranged from five feet, six inches and 155 pounds to six feet and 190 pounds.

The Strongside Guard. The strongside guard in the Pro-I is the strongest and biggest of the two guards as most plays are run at him and the strongside tackle. He is required to block more area than the weakside guard and should be able to trap either in or out. In addition, pulling for sweeps is important in this position, although not as much as on the weakside. The guards on our squads have averaged between 180 and 200 pounds. If we have two guards of equal ability, we will put the taller of the two on the strongside to give the offensive line the look of being strongside. (This would also be the case in deciding between two tackles of equal ability.)

The Center. The center in the Multiple Pro-I offense is not the smallest man in the line, but neither is he the biggest, because the position is not necessarily so physically demanding. He can always get help on a big nose guard by double teaming him with one of the offensive guards, for instance. Also, we do not require that our center be able to snap punts or extra points. We feel that some other player could take over these duties if necessary. This, of course, is a matter of preference. The center does, however, have to be quick. He is able to make cut blocks on the defensive lineman on the side where the play is called and is quick enough to make blocks on the middle linebacker as well as screen block and double team on the nose guard. Agility, also, is helpful in making these cut off blocks. Our centers range between 180 and 195 pounds.

PRO-I RECEIVERS

Split End and Flanker. The requirements for split end and flanker are usually the same in that both have speed enough for the deep routes and have good hands and the ability to get the ball under pressure. They are agile and have the determination to catch the long passes as well as run the curl pattern, one of our favorites. We put our best receiver at the split end because he is on the line of scrimmage and can get deeper faster—and usually has one-on-one coverage because the strongside is away from him. We take advantage of the quickness of the wide receiver by throwing short patterns to him such as swings, hitches, stops, or look-ins. It is possible with the Pro-I offense to put both wide receivers on the same side by using the slot formation discussed in Chapter 1. The flanker will run a combination pattern with both the split ends and tight end; so this position could be manned by a slightly slower individual than the split end. In one year, using these guidelines, our three receivers caught 27, 28, and 23 passes for close to 1,500 yards while two running backs also gained 1,500 yards in rushing.

The blocking required for these positions is a crack back block on the line of scrimmage or a downfield screen block. Size, therefore, is not as important for this reason as is the ability to be able to catch the football.

Tight End. The tight end for the Multiple Pro-I is a good blocker as most plays are to the strongside. Physically, he should be the strongest of the receivers because of double team blocks with the tackle or blocking down on the defensive tackle or linebacker. His ability to catch the football will greatly add to the passing attack. We use the tight end on "under" patterns such as delays, drags, swings, or hooks. We can send him deep depending on the tight end's speed. One tight end at Marcos de Niza caught ten passes for us in one year in part-time duty for five touchdowns. In addition, our school record for catches in one year is held by a tight end. We have been blessed with unusually tall tight ends—six feet, three inches to six feet, five inches—and one went on to play as a freshman at a major Midwestern university.

PRO-I BACKFIELD

The Quarterback. The Multiple Pro-I quarterback, besides possessing the general characteristics indicative of almost all offenses—leadership, respect, maturity, intelligence, enthusiasm, confidence, and common sense—must also be the best passer on the team, with quick hands, quick feet, and an above-average throwing arm. Height here is not a prerequisite. However, our quarterbacks have passed for over 1,200 yards in a season at Marcos de Niza using this offense. Running ability in quarterbacks is more a matter of fear than a designed play. The Pro-I offense, as we run it, has our quarterbacks helping the team more by passing than running.

The Fullback. The fullback is the best blocker in the backfield for the Multiple Pro-I because he will be the lead blocker for the tailback who carries the ball most of the time. In addition, he is the strongest of the two running backs for this offense because of the inside running game involved. He must be determined enough and have the necessary strength to get tough yardage. Ruggedness, durability, aggressiveness, and good hands, if the coach is planning to throw to the backs, are all pluses here. Our fullbacks have ranged in size from five feet, six inches and 155 pounds to six feet two inches and 195 pounds. The size of the smallest fullback still did not keep him from being the best blocker on the team. We have had a very quick fullback and a "lumbering" fullback; and both did equally well because the play calling in this offense is easily adjusted to take care of either type of runner. Regardless of his running ability, our main concern here is still the ability to block because of the fullback's lead blocking for the tailback and blocking for any defensive end on our roll back passes.

The Tailback. The tailback for the Multiple Pro-I is the best runner in the backfield because he will be carrying the ball most of the time. In addition, he should have good hands for receiving because he has regular pass patterns as well as screen patterns to handle. His durability and strength will be tested with the inside game we have set up for him and his outside speed by the sweep which we have in the offense. Any outstanding blocking ability and passing ability will be considered a bonus and definitely taken advantage of. We have had two tailbacks that have gained over 1,200 yards in the past by using this offense. They have been relatively short, the tallest being five feet, ten inches, and the heaviest being 175 pounds. You can see, then, that outright size is not really a prerequisite for this position. However, quickness and good acceleration to control the inside and outside running game and insure a deep threat in passing situations are extremely important. The tailback needs strength to be able to run inside and speed to be able to run outside.

3

HOW TO COACH
PROPER STANCE
AND SPACING
FOR THE PRO-I OFFENSE

After several years of trial and error, a spacing and positioning philosophy has been developed which we feel is right for the Pro-I offense. We try to keep the gaps in the line the same whether we are running against a stunting defense or a reading defense. We do this to keep the same visual appearance for all our plays. The only time we vary from this positioning in the line is when we are near the goal line. Then we tighten up the offensive line into an almost foot-to-foot positioning. (The receivers and running backs still keep their basic positioning no matter what the split in the line may be.)

PROPER STANCE AND SPACING

Linemen: There is a two to three foot split between the guards and the center and a one yard split between the guard and tackle in the Pro-I. Hands are placed down as close as possible to the neutral zone for the linemen *(Diagram 3–1)*.

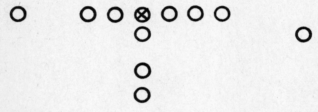

Diagram 3–1

Receivers: Depending on the play, one to three yard split separates the tight end from the tackle on his side in the Pro-I. The split end is eight to ten yards from the tackle and the flanker is five to ten yards outside the tight end, two yards off the ball. All splits vary if the receiver has to block back on the line of scrimmage *(Diagram 3–1)*.

Running Backs: The fullback's hand is placed down four and a half to five yards off the ball in all formations. Position of the stance in the I set is directly behind the center and quarterback. Any formation that puts the fullback in an off-center alignment means that he straddles the inside leg of the tackle on that side. The tailback in the I set is one to two yards behind the fullback in a stand-up position. Hands may be on the knees or on top of the thigh pads. In any other formation, his hand is on the ground four and a half to five yards off the ball, straddling the inside leg of the tackle on that side *(Diagram 3–1)*.

FEET IN RELATION TO HIPS AND SHOULDERS AND WEIGHT DISTRIBUTION

Linemen: In the lineman's stance, we put the hand as close as possible to the neutral zone, placing the head directly above or slightly behind the hand. This prevents the lineman from being off-side. The feet should be approximately shoulder's width apart so that he is comfortable. Too narrow a stance eliminates power; too wide a stance reduces lateral movement. We start with a heel-toe relationship, with the feet flat on the ground and weight back toward the heel of the foot. Ninety percent of the weight will be on the feet and only ten percent on the hands. This weight distribution eliminates discoloration on the hand from too much weight forward (a condition which might show the direction of the charge) and serves as a spring effect with the weight toward the heels. The larger players can put one leg back further but still maintain a flat foot with the weight back. The head must be up so the lineman can see the linebacker's knees. This will force the tail down and the back at a downward angle, placing more weight at the back of the stance.

By using this stance and the spring effect, we feel the offensive lineman can control the line of scrimmage by exploding across the neutral zone. This stance also does not hinder any cross blocking, trapping, pulling, or pass blocking. The center will have the feet balanced and flat with more weight forward on the football because of his position. We use the quarter turn snap, popping the ball into the quarterback's hand with the laces across the fingers of his throwing hand. Both hands should be on the ball prior to the snap.

Receivers: The tight end's stance and weight distribution will be the same as the interior linemen. This is because of his blocking assignment along the line of scrimmage. The wide receivers have no special stance. They can run either from a two point or a three point depending on what is comfortable to the individual. The main thing we do ask is that they be consistent in their choice of stances. If we are playing on a wet field, we would rather have our wide receivers operate from a two point stance.

Running Backs: The fullback and tailback (when in a three point) will have the same basic stance. All the weight is on the feet, which are flat on the ground. No weight at all is on the hand. The weight on the feet is shifted toward the back to be able to give him a good start in all directions. Keeping the feet flat also helps to eliminate the false step backward used by many running backs. The head of the running back can be down. We have found that keeping the head up in his stance has no real advantage or disadvantage in his ability to run to daylight. He knows what hole he should hit when the ball is snapped and where his blockers are coming from, and he should be able to adjust when he approaches the hole. This also eliminates "pointing" since some have a tendency to look where they are going to run before the ball is snapped.

Quarterback: The quarterback's feet are placed shoulder width apart, with feet flat but weight forward on the balls of the feet. His back is as erect as possible so he can see the defense. In finding the correct position for the quarterback, it is important above all that he feel comfortable.

4

HOW TO ESTABLISH
OFFENSIVE LINE
BLOCKING RULES

INITIATING A NUMBERING SYSTEM
IN NAMING BLOCKS

The numbering system used in this Multiple Pro-I offense was started at Charleroi High School in Pennsylvania back in the 1950's under coach ''Rab'' Currie. Calls were then added or eliminated as the offense evolved until this final form resulted.

The calls used in the numbering system will be used on every play so that the defense cannot key on any one player if he makes a call at the line of scrimmage. By initiating a numbering system in naming blocks, the coach will find it easier to communicate with the linemen in terms of numbers instead of block descriptions. Isn't it easier, for instance, to say, "Why didn't you 1 block?" instead of, "Why didn't you run the trap block to the outside?" Also, since the plays in the Pro-I are descriptive, the number cannot be confused with the hole, such as on a dive right 3 block. Finally, it is much easier to call a block or change a block at the line of scrimmage when a numbering system is used. With this in mind, here are the blocking patterns used in the Multiple Pro-I.

0 (Zero) Block. The 0 block is a cross block between the tackle and the end with the free man or outside man going first *(Diagram 4–1)*.

Diagram 4–1

The block is used mainly for off tackle plays, giving the offensive line a different way of blocking the off tackle hole, and it is useful when attacking the defensive tackle from a different angle rather than one-on-one all the time. It may be used if you have a particularly strong tight end that can handle a defensive tackle.

Tackle Responsibilities: If the tackle goes first, this means that there is a linebacker on him. The tackle must step directly at the defensive end, cutting off his penetration to the inside by putting his head across the front. By using this block, the tackle can "ride" the defensive end to the outside away from the off tackle hole. If the end goes first, this means there is a down lineman on the offensive tackle. The tackle's responsibility here is to drop step, thus clearing the offensive end, then step directly at the defensive end using the same techniques mentioned above.

End Responsibilities: If the end goes first, it means a down lineman is on the offensive tackle. The offensive end must cut off penetration of the defensive tackle by stepping directly at him, sliding his head across the front, and driving the defensive tackle down the line using the shoulder. This must be accompanied by the defensive end or the 0 block will break down. If the tackle goes first, the end will drop step around the offensive tackle and attack the linebacker, taking him in any direction that he can and letting the running back run to daylight. We do not ask our linemen to block a linebacker in any specific direction but let him take him in whatever direction he wants to go.

Coaching Point: A coaching point for this block as well as others mentioned in this chapter is that the blocker should step directly at the man who is to be blocked, sliding the head to the position where the defensive man must be cut off and making firm contact with the shoulder, keeping the feet wide apart and maintaining proper balance. Contact must also be maintained throughout the block.

1 Block. The 1 block is a short trap to the outside and is another way of blocking the off tackle hole *(Diagram 4–2)*. This block is particularly useful if you have a good trapping guard and a tight end strong enough to handle the defensive tackle. We use this block to give another blocking pattern at the hole and get a running back through the hole to act as an extra blocker.

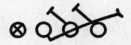

Diagram 4–2

End Responsibility: The end must block the first man to his inside on or off the line of scrimmage. If the defensive man is on the line of scrimmage, this block would basically be the same as the 0 block discussed above. If a linebacker is the first man to the inside, the end must make sure the linebacker is not blitzing and also must be able to handle a scraping or shuffling linebacker. His main responsibility is to make certain the penetration of the defensive man is cut off at the line of scrimmage so that the trapping guard does not have to run around him or his block. He can control the linebacker by any effective method he deems necessary, including the shoulder block (if the linebacker is blitzing), cutting the linebacker down at the knees using the cut block, or a screen block if the linebacker happens to step the wrong way or is out of position.

Tackle Responsibility: The tackle must also block the first man to the inside on or off the line of scrimmage. If the defensive man is down, the tackle must cut off penetration by stepping directly at him, getting the head across in front, and driving him down the line using his shoulder. If a linebacker is to the inside, he can use any of the methods described above for the offensive end.

Guard Responsibility: The guard on the 1 block is responsible for trapping the first man outside of the tight end's block. He will take a drop step to clear the offensive tackle and approach the defensive man, usually the end, at a good IOB angle. If the defensive man is penetrating, the block should be made with the head in front of the man (the offensive side of the line of scrimmage), riding him to the outside. If the defensive man is reading, the head should go on the defensive side of the man, using the shoulder block. A good route and proper balance are the keys to the guard's correct execution of the 1 block.

Running Back Responsibilities: The running back is included in the 1 block because he does have certain responsibilities when it is called. His blocking route is through the hole which would be on the outside leg of the tight end and inside the man being trapped, looking to the inside to help block any linebacker. The running back should go through the hole after the guard has made his block. We realize that an angle block on a linebacker sitting off the ball is a very difficult block for any offensive lineman, and this is the reason we have the running back looking to the inside to help block under these circumstances.

2 Block. The 2 block is a cross block between a guard and a tackle with the outside or three man going first *(Diagram 4–3)*. This block is used on counter plays to the inside and is another way of blocking the defensive tackle on a play that is run inside of him. It is of particular use when the offensive linemen have good quickness or agility.

Diagram 4–3

Tackle Responsibility: If the tackle goes first, it means there is a down lineman on the offensive guard. The tackle must step directly at the man, getting his head across the front, blocking with the shoulder, and driving the man down the line of scrimmage. He must cut off penetration. If the guard goes first, the tackle must drop step to clear the guard and attack the linebacker blocking him in any direction that he wants to go.

Guard Responsibilities: If the guard goes first, it means there is a linebacker on him. He must step straight at the defensive tackle, getting the head in front of him, blocking him with the shoulder, and driving him to the outside. The defensive tackle must not penetrate to the football. If the tackle goes first, the guard must drop step, clear the tackle, and attack the defensive man according to the defense being played. If a defensive lineman is on the tackle, his blocking angle must stop the penetration to the inside while turning him to the outside. If a linebacker is on the offensive tackle, he must attack the linebacker and block him any way the linebacker wants to go.

3 Block. The 3 block is the basic one-on-one block used for any offensive running play—especially when the offensive line can overpower the defense or when the backs are quick enough to employ a screen type of block. Everyone at the point of attack will use the same rule on this block, namely the BAS *(Diagram 4-4)*.

4 Block. The 4 block is used basically against a gap type of defense where everyone in the offensive line blocks down or back toward the ball. The main job of the offensive lineman in each case is to cut off the penetration from the defensive lineman by putting his head in front of the defender and driving him down the line of scrimmage with a shoulder block. The center may either block the middle linebacker or away from the play, depending on the discretion of the coach *(Diagram 4-5)*.

Diagram 4-4   *Diagram 4-5*

5 Block. The 5 block is a cross between the center and the hole side guard and is only used against odd man fronts. (Against even defenses, this block would be part of the trapping game and would be called by a different name.) The guard will go first, putting his head in front of the nose guard and blocking him with his shoulder away from the play while the center will drop step around the guard and attack the linebacker head on, letting the back run to daylight. This block is excellent for use on such plays as a counter, draws, or some other type of delayed running pattern in the backfield *(Diagram 4-6)*.

22 Block. The 22 block is a double team between the tight end and the tackle used when a power type of block is needed on an off tackle running play *(Diagram 4-7)*.

Diagram 4-6   *Diagram 4-7*

Tackle's Responsibility: The tackle's responsibility is to act as a post man on the double team. He must stop the penetration of the defensive tackle by firing out and neutralizing the defender in the neutral zone of the line of scrimmage. His head will be placed on the hole side of the defender while blocking with the shoulder. If the defender tries to go inside, a reverse body block may be used to cut off this route. The tackle must also try to drive the defender back so his legs and feet are out of the running lane.

End Responsibility: The end's responsibility is to act as the lead man on the double team block. His head will be to the back side of the defender at the hip, and he will make contact with his shoulder, trying to drive the defender off the ball. He will move his body toward the offensive tackle to eliminate the defensive tackle splitting the double team. If the tackle tries to roll toward the hole, the defender's head will be in perfect position to stop this defensive maneuver. The end must also strive to get his legs and feet out of the running lane. When attacking the defensive tackle, if his hip disappears to the inside (which means the defensive tackle is slanting away from him), he will continue inside and block the next defender, usually an inside linebacker *(Diagram 4-8)*.

Diagram 4-8

55 Block. The 55 block is a double team between the center and the hole side guard, basically used on trap running plays versus an odd man front. We gave this block a name because it is not always necessary to double team a nose guard. If we want the center to block a defender away from the hole on a particular play, the 55 block will not be used. It is used only when we want a double team on the nose guard *(Diagram 4–9)*.

Diagram 4–9

Center's Responsibility: The center is the post man on the double team, his main responsibility being to stop penetration of the nose guard by firing out and neutralizing the defender in the neutral zone of the line of scrimmage, just as the tackle does in the 22 block. His head will also be placed on the hole side of the defender while blocking with the shoulder, and he will use a reverse body block to cut off the route if the defender tries to go around. He will also attempt to drive the defender back to get his legs and feet out of the running lane.

Guard's Responsibility: The guard's responsibilities on the 55 block are much the same as end responsibilities on the 22 block. On the 55 block, the guard will act as the lead man on the double team block, his head to the back side of the defender at the hip, making contact with his shoulder to drive the defender off the ball. He will move his body toward the offensive center to eliminate the defensive nose guard trying to split the double team, and he is responsible for getting his legs and feet out of the running lane. If the nose guard slants away, he will continue and block the next defender, usually a linebacker.

CHANGING THE BLOCK AT THE LINE OF SCRIMMAGE

The blocks in the Pro-I offense are called in the huddle along with the play and seldom are changed at the line of scrimmage. If an occasion arises however, when the block called in the huddle will not work because of a different defense, we make provisions so that the lineman can change the block at the line of scrimmage. The two tackles and the center are responsible for changing the block when the play is being run at them. To keep the defense from keying on these people, all offensive linemen are asked to make some type of call at the line of scrimmage. If the lineman at the point of attack wants to change the blocking pattern, his call will not be the only one being made at the line. The only problem which might arise is making sure the point of attack called is made in such a manner that everybody hears the call. For example, if an off tackle play with a 22 block is called in the huddle, and the defensive formation is such that a 22 block will not work, the offensive tackle on that side can call "1." The call must be made loud enough so that the two linemen on either side and the fullback will hear it. The fullback, meanwhile, knows that he must be listening for any changes at the line of scrimmage and will block out all calls except the one coming from the play side tackle. If the play side tackle makes a dummy call, that is, any number not in our blocking system, then everyone knows the block called in the huddle will be run. It is possible to have the quarterback change the call at the line of scrimmage if he knows the offense well enough to do this. In this case, only the quarterback's call would have the authority to change the block. (On plays that are run on the quick count, no calls are made.)

5

HOW TO COACH THE INSIDE RUNNING GAME IN THE MULTIPLE PRO-I OFFENSE

During the past few years it has become apparent to those involved with the Pro-I offense that using descriptive terminology to call the offensive running game has several advantages. First, it enables the players to locate the hole more easily. It eliminates hole numbering, play cards and certain blocking for certain plays at a certain hole. The plays used in the Pro-I running game, therefore, have been broken down into the areas shown in *Diagram 5–1*. By using this diagram, the player knows that a dive right will go over the outside leg of the guard regardless of which running back carries the football. The back carrying the ball will be controlled by calling fullback dive right or tailback dive right. With this in mind then, let's look at the inside running game of the Multiple Pro-I offense.

The inside running game of the Pro-I offense takes advantage of the quickness and ability of the running backs to run from tackle to tackle. It also uses to full advantage outstanding linemen and can be adapted to run against any defense by using specific blocking patterns that will be described later.

Diagram 5–1

THE DIVE

The first play in the inside running game is the basis for almost all running games—the dive. The dive, according to the offensive chart in *Diagram 5–1*, is run over the outside leg of the guard. The back carrying the football will be designated by the call in the huddle. For example, fullback dive right will send the fullback over the outside leg of the guard on the right side *(Diagram 5–2)*.

The quarterback's technique on the dive is to step backward toward the fullback, looking the ball into the fullback's belt and giving the ball to the fullback in a short, riding motion as the fullback attacks the line of scrimmage. After the ball is given to the fullback, the quarterback continues down the line, faking the option.

The tailback's technique is to get out of the way. He lines up in any formation and goes in any direction as long as he does not interfere with the fullback.

Different formations can also be used to send the different backs at the different dive routes. For example, with a white formation tailback dive left, the tailback carries the ball over the outside leg of the guard on the left side *(Diagram 5–3)*. The brown formation tailback dive left is the same as the white formation except for the fullback's position.

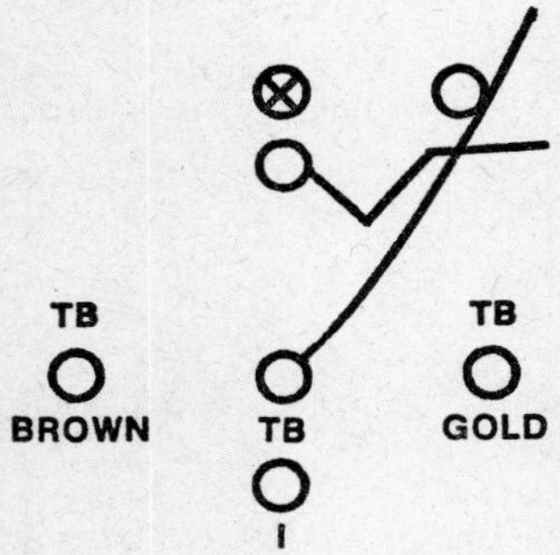

Diagram 5–2 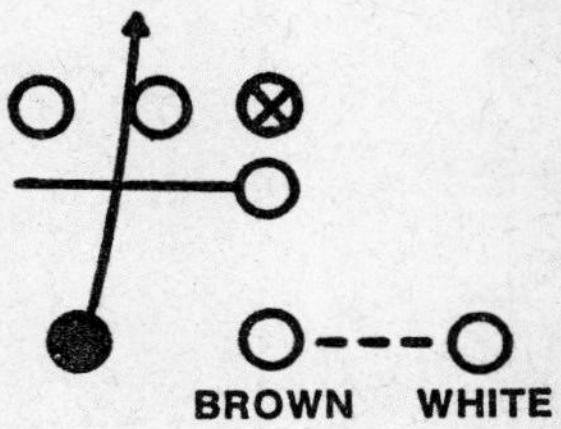　　　　　　　　　　　　　　　　*Diagram 5–3*

The gold formation tailback dive right positions the tailback in a right halfback position *(Diagram 5–4)*. In addition, the fullback dive right or left can be run from either of the last two formations.

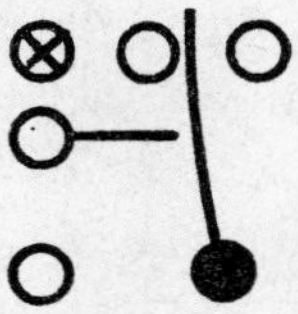

Diagram 5–4

Finally, a good short yardage dive would employ the tailback dive right (or left) fullback lead. In this play, the fullback would lead through the hole, picking up the first off color jersey that appeared *(Diagram 5-5)*.

Diagram 5-5

BLOCKING THE DIVES

Regardless of the defense used by the opposing team, one of the following blocking schemes should enable the offense to persevere. For example, the best blocking pattern used for this running play, because of the quickness of the running back, will be the 3 block. The key block here will obviously come from the guard since the back is running at him; and the guard, therefore, takes the linebacker or down lineman in any direction the defensive player wants to go. The running back will follow the guard's helmet, and the center and offensive tackle on the side of the hole will turn their linemen or linebacker away from the hole. The other linemen and wide receivers will be sent to the running lane. Players are not assigned a specific downfield block, but the blocker is sent into the running lane, blocking off colored jerseys. This eliminates looking for a certain defensive back downfield *(Diagram 5-6)*.

Another blocking pattern useful in the Pro-I dive is the 2 block. This block can be used with quick offensive linemen cross blocking in front of the running back *(Diagram 5-7)*.

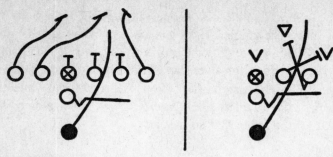

Diagram 5-6   Diagram 5-7

Finally, a third blocking scheme, especially successful in a short yardage situation, is the wedge block. In this case, the wedge would be formed on the guard *(Diagram 5-8)*.

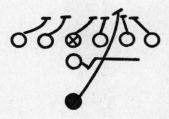

Diagram 5-8

THE COUNTER

The counter, sister play to the dive, has enjoyed much success at Marcos de Niza since its inception four years ago. It is extremely effective with a fullback who runs the dive with authority, and our tailbacks have each gained over 1,000 yards, roughly fifty percent of which can be attributed to this play.

The basic counter is run from the I over the outside leg of the guard. The quarterback fakes the dive, turns his back to the line of scrimmage to hand the ball to the tailback, then drops back and fake passes. The fullback's route will be opposite the call. His job will be to fake the dive. The tailback takes one step opposite the call, turns his head and shoulders to indicate a play to the outside, then steps back and runs his route up over the guard. For example, tailback counter left will send the fullback over the right side while the tailback will go over the left side *(Diagram 5–9)*. *Note:* a drop step can be used by the tailback if so desired.

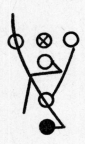

Diagram 5–9

Other formations in which the counters can be run are brown formation tailback counter left *(Diagram 5–10)*, brown formation fullback counter right *(Diagram 5–11)*, gold formation tailback counter right *(Diagram 5–12)*, gold formation fullback counter left *(Diagram 5–13)*, white formation tailback counter left *(Diagram 5–14)*, and white formation fullback counter right *(Diagram 5–15)*.

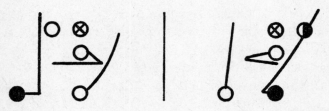

Diagram 5–10   *Diagram 5–11*

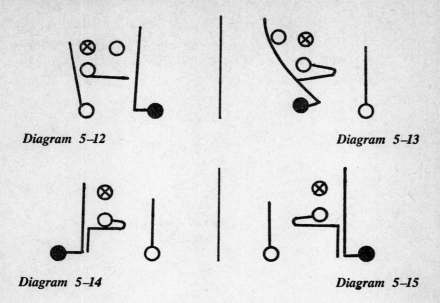

Diagram 5–12   Diagram 5–13

Diagram 5–14   Diagram 5–15

BLOCKING THE COUNTER

The most successful blocking pattern used with the counter is the 2 block. We found this to be true because of the blocking angles that our offensive linemen get on the defense—for example, in the tailback counter left 2 block *(Diagram 5–16)*.

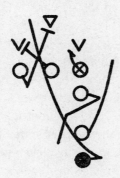

Diagram 5–16

In addition, the play may be blocked with the 3 block and by trap blocking. The 3 block is good because the offensive linemen are blocking straight ahead while the trap block may be used if you have a good trapping game *(Diagram 5–17)*.

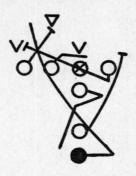

Diagram 5–17   **Tailback Counter Left Trap Blocking**

COACHING THE SLANTS

The slant is a play designed to run off tackle while giving the appearance in the beginning of a sweep. This play takes advantage of the tailback's running ability and particularly his ability to pick his own hole, that is, run to daylight. Since the slant has become so popular with our tailbacks, we wanted to make sure that we could block it different ways to keep the defense from reading the play. There is a possibility of four blocking patterns, and any of the four can be used to take advantage of the offensive linemen's skills, a defensive weakness, or just the ability to run against a certain defense. The play may be exceptionally good against a fast pursuing defense or a defense in which the defensive ends charge hard across the line of scrimmage. The backfield routes of the fullback are determined by the blocking pattern called either in the huddle or at the line of scrimmage, and he must pay close attention to the offensive lineman on the side of the play if the block is changed at the line of scrimmage.

BLOCKING THE SLANT

Since we have a strong side with a tight end and a weak side with a split end, the fullback's rule may vary slightly depending on the direction of the play. For example, on a 22 block on the strong side, the fullback must attack the defensive end on the inside out route using what we call a J-block (discussed in Chapter 1). His responsibility on this blocking pattern is to block the defensive end outside. On a 1, 0, or 3 block, he will round off his route and lead through the hole looking to help to the inside *(Diagram 5–18)*. On the weak side, the only blocking pattern that could be run would be a 3 block. The fullback's responsibility in this case is to J-block the defensive end. *Note:* if the tight end goes left, or a wingback left is used, all strong side blocking rules can be initiated—for example, tight left, slant left 22 block *(Diagram 5–19)* or wing left, slant left 22 block *(Diagram 5–20)*.

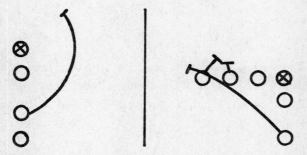

Diagram 5–18 Round Off Route   **Diagram 5–19**

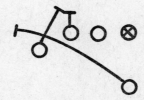

Diagram 5–20

The quarterback's responsibility in the slant is to put the ball, once the snap is taken, on the hip so that the defensive end being run at cannot see the ball. The quarterback's route will be a 45° angle toward the side of the attack. As he approaches the tailback, he gets the ball into a handoff position and gives the ball to the tailback at a depth of anywhere from four to seven yards behind the line of scrimmage, depending on how deep the tailback lines up. The tailback's route is an open, cross, plant, square up technique. As he squares up, he receives the ball from the quarterback and uses his blocking accordingly *(Diagram 5–21)*.

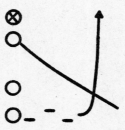

Diagram 5–21

The variations of the slant are tailback slant right 22 block *(Diagram 5–22)*, tailback slant right 1 block *(Diagram 5–23)*, tailback slant right 0 block *(Diagram 5–24)*, and tailback slant left 3

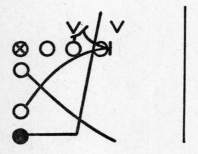

Diagram 5–22

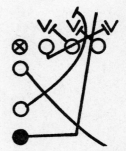

Diagram 5–23

block *(Diagram 5–25)*, tight left, slant left 22 block *(Diagram 5–26)*, and wing left, slant left 22 block *(Diagram 5–27)*.

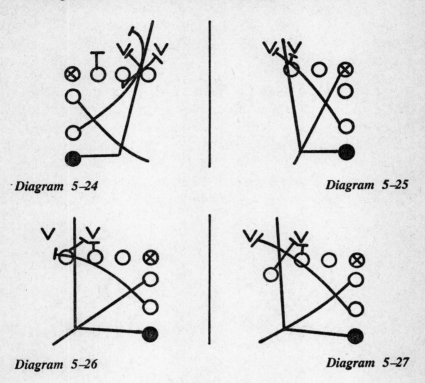

Diagram 5–24

Diagram 5–25

Diagram 5–26

Diagram 5–27

THE SLIPS

The slips are used to take advantage of the fullback's lateral running ability. The play is designed to go off tackle, using the same blocking schemes as the slants. It is an excellent quick hitting play for the fullback and could very easily be adjusted to go outside to take advantage of any defensive positioning.

The fullback's route for the slips is to the outside leg of the tackle *(Diagram 5–28)*. He receives the ball from the quarterback and reads the blocks of the linemen in front of him.

Diagram 5–28

   The quarterback's route is reverse pivot to the hole, getting the ball to the fullback as soon as possible. The tailback's position must be so that he can lead the fullback through the hole. The tailback's route will depend on the blocking pattern called such as, in the gold formation fullback slip right 1 block *(Diagram 5–29)*. *Note:* The tailback must J-block using the same rule as the fullback on the slant, for instance on the brown fullback slip left 3 block in *Diagram 5–30*.

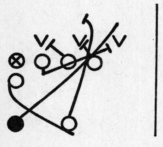

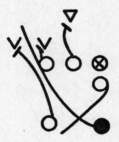

Diagram 5–29   *Diagram 5–30*

6

THE TRAPPING GAME

The trapping game, as far as the running attack is concerned, is separated in the Pro-I offense because a different type of blocking is used. The running routes are set up so that the lineman can get better blocking angles at the defense. By using the blocking rules in this chapter, the lineman can handle any trap. Formations and the ball carrier mean little. The lineman knows only if it is a trap left or a trap right. This also enables the coaches to use their imagination, do a little daydreaming with the pencil, and come up with different backfield patterns without changing any lineman blocking rules.

COACHING THE CORRECT TRAP RUNNING ROUTES

The center will be the focal point for all trap running routes in the Pro-I. When a trap right is called in the I formation, the correct running route for the running back will be to start for the left leg of the center then bend to the right following the trapper. In the brown or white formation, the running back's route is a straight line through the center from left to right. This is true no matter who carries the ball or from what formation *(Diagrams 6–1, 6–2, & 6–3)*. The same would be true on a trap left call except that the running back will head for the right leg of the center then adjust his route by following the trapper. The formation or running back will make no difference in this rule *(Diagrams 6–4, 6–5, & 6–6)*. *Note:* The fullback's route from the I formation is a little more bent than the other running back position because of the angle needed to set up the trap block.

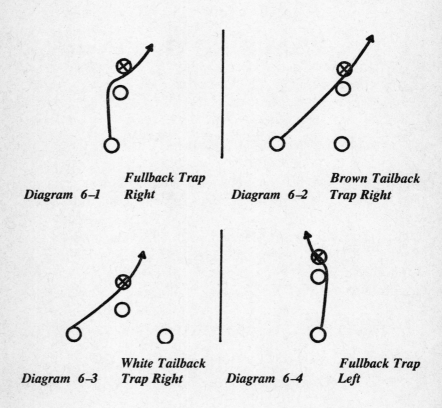

Diagram 6–1	**Fullback Trap Right**	*Diagram 6–2*	**Brown Tailback Trap Right**
Diagram 6–3	**White Tailback Trap Right**	*Diagram 6–4*	**Fullback Trap Left**

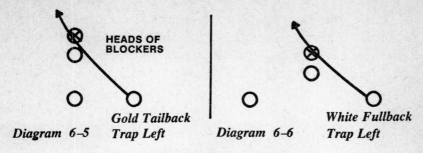

Diagram 6–5 Gold Tailback Trap Left

Diagram 6–6 White Fullback Trap Left

DOUBLE TEAM BLOCK

The double team block is called the 55 block *(Diagram 4–9)*, which is used on the nose guard in the trapping game. The double team is used when a big nose guard must be neutralized or driven back or when a nose guard is quick and must be kept out of the running lane. The center's responsibility, as the post blocker, is to neutralize the charge of the noseguard, keep the noseguard from driving him back, and, if possible, drive the nose guard back while getting his legs and feet out of the running lane. His head will be on the hole side of the nose guard. If the nose guard tries to roll away from the double team, the center can ride him away or use a reverse body block. The guard will be the lead man and clean block or screen block the nose guard. His responsibility is to close the gap between the center and himself by moving his body in that direction. His block will be on the hip of the nose guard with his head on the backside. If the nose guard tries to split the seam, his body will cut the nose guard off. If the nose guard tries to roll into the play, the guard's head will be in perfect position to prevent this *(Diagrams 6–7, 6–8, & 6–9)*.

Diagram 6–7 Correct Head Position

Diagram 6–8 Correct Body Position

Diagram 6–9 Reverse Body Block

If the nose guard being double teamed slants away from the lead guard and his hip disappears, the lead guard will continue his same route and block the next man, usually the linebacker *(Diagram 6–10)*. (The drills run for this block are called two-on-one and double team.)

Diagram 6–10

SUBA

The SUBA (Set Up Block Away) block is used only in our trapping game. The block can be practiced by itself, usually before or after practice or as part of the whole trapping game. (We use the whole trapping game to practice this particular block.) How much and when the block is used during a game will depend on the type of offense that is used, but for our purposes it is utilized for an influence block on the man that is being trapped. The offensive lineman must know who is going to be trapped and thus use the block to its greatest potential.

We trap the first down man on the play side *(Diagrams 6–11, & 6–12)*.

Diagram 6–11   *Trap Left*

Diagram 6–12   **Trap Right**

Once the defensive linemen know who is to be trapped, the SUBA block is used. It is not an aggressive block so that the lineman gets tangled up with the defensive man; nor is it so passive that the defender neglects him. It must be made, however, with enough force to get the defender's attention to the outside part of his body, that is, away from the ball *(Diagram 6–13)*.

Diagram 6–13

This maneuver will give the defender the first thought of a play coming to his outside. After the initial hit, the SUBA blocker will then turn his back to the hole and block the first defender to the outside *(Diagrams 6–14 & 6–15)*.

Diagram 6–14   *Diagram 6–15*

If the defender has taken himself out of the play, the SUBA blocker will then turn and get into the running lane to block *(Diagram 6–16)*.

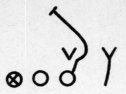

Diagram 6-16

BIB BLOCKING

The BIB block (Block Inside Backer) is used to take advantage of the best angle for blocking the linebacker. It is also run as part of our whole trapping game but can be run separately. The BIB blocker is the next offensive lineman to the outside of the SUBA blocker. The BIB block is best made when the offensive lineman scrapes as close as possible to the defender who is to be trapped. The block on the linebacker will be made at the hip with the head in front of him. If the linebacker is setting or going backward, the block should be made with ease. Difficulty will result if the linebacker steps up into the hole. In this case, the correct blocking route becomes very important because it is the responsibility of the BIB blocker to root the linebacker out of the running lane *(Diagrams 6-17, 6-18 & 6-19)*. The BIB blocker will have time to go inside because of the delay taken by the SUBA blocker.

Diagram 6-17    *Diagram 6-18*

Diagram 6-19

If the guard SUBAs in this offense, the tackle will BIB. If the tackle SUBAs, the end will BIB. Between these two offensive linemen (SUBA and BIB), one must block the linebacker and one must block the first defender outside of the trap block *(Diagrams 6–20 & 6–21)*.

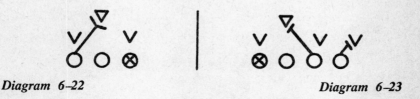

Diagram 6–20    *Diagram 6–21*

The only time a SUBA-BIB combo cannot be used is on the split end side against a five man front defense. The tackle in this case cannot SUBA because there is no BIB man to his outside; therefore he would BIB *(Diagram 6–22)*.

Switches may be called to help block the linebacker if the linebacker is playing up-tight and the regular BIB block cannot get him. A switch in assignments is called by the two offensive linemen involved or the coach *(Diagram 6–23)*.

Diagram 6–22   *Diagram 6–23*

CORRECT TRAPPING ROUTES

The correct trapping route for the guards is an important part of the trapping game. If all other blocks are made or missed, usually yardage will depend on whether the trap block is made. The best drill used for the guards in these routes involves placing three dummy holders at three different positions where the defenders could be, kneeling and facing the guard. On the snap count, the guard pulls and one of the defenders stands and is trapped. Placing the defenders at different depths causes the trapper to get a good IOB (Inside Out Block) angle *(Diagram 6–24)*. The type of block used will depend on where the defender will be. Number one will be with the head on the offensive side of the line of scrimmage (left shoulder in this case). Number three will be with the head on the defensive side of the line of scrimmage (right shoulder in this case). Number two would be a personal choice for the coach. It may change week to week depending on the type of defense the other team plays. A reading defense may take a right shoulder block whereas an aggressive defense will take a left shoulder block. The important thing to remember is the correct route the guard must take to be in position to make the block.

Diagram 6–24

TRAPPING GAME SYNOPSIS

The total trapping picture can be seen in *Diagrams 6–25 & 6–26*.

Trap Right

WT—BAS	SG—Lead, SUBA
WG—Trap	ST—SUBA, BIB
C—MOMA	TE—BIB, BAS

Even

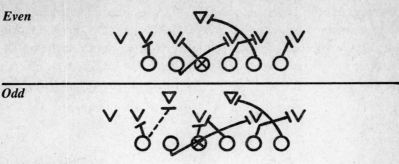

Odd

Diagram 6–25

Trap Left

WT—BIB   SG—Trap
WG—Lead, SUBA   ST—BAS
C—MOMA   TE—BAS

Even

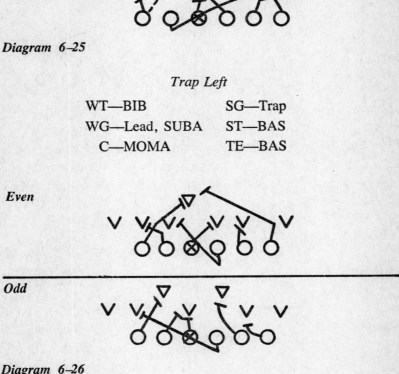

Odd

Diagram 6–26

FOLD BLOCK

The fold block is another type of trap that may be used against a defense that reads very well and may not take to false keys (that is, SUBA block). Also, if they have a very good linebacker, we change the responsibility of the trapping guard and the offensive man playing opposite the defender normally being trapped. The trapper will fold around the center and block the linebacker head on, taking him in any direction he can. It is up to the back to run to daylight. The trapper will be receiving help from the BIB blocker so in effect a double team will take place on the linebacker *(Diagrams 6–27 & 6–28)*.

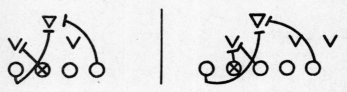

Diagram 6–27   *Diagram 6–28*

The SUBA blocker must now block the defender on him one-on-one and turn the defender away from the hole *(Diagrams 6–29 & 6–30)*. The complete fold block will then look like *Diagrams 6–31 & 6–32*.

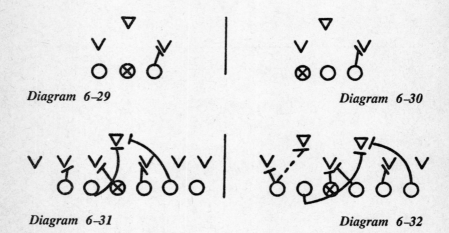

Diagram 6–29   *Diagram 6–30*

Diagram 6–31   *Vs.*   *Diagram 6–32*

**Trap Right Fold   Trap Right Fold
Block–Even Defense   Block–Odd Defense**

TACKLE TRAPS

The tackle trap gives a slightly different look to the defense as far as the trapping game is concerned. A different player is trapping (the tackle) and the play usually will take longer to develop because of the distance the tackle has to travel. The backfield action will usually be some type of counter or delay. It is also a good trapping play against a 4-4 defense. No special drills are needed, but the tackles must now be schooled on the IOB angle. The terminology will remain the same, and no matter who carries the ball from what formation, the lineman rules will be the same. One change for the backs will be that the other running back *should* fill for the pulling tackle *(Diagrams 6–33 & 6–34)*.

Tackle Trap Right

WT—Trap	SG—Lead, SUBA
C—BAS	ST—SUBA, BIB
WG—BAS	TE—BIB, BAS

Even

Odd

Diagram 6–33

Tackle Trap Left

WT—BIB	SG—BAS
WG—Lead, SUBA	ST—Trap
C—BAS	TE—Running lane

Even

Odd

Diagram 6-34

If a double team is not wanted on the nose guard, the lead man could block BAS and produce a possible double team on the linebacker *(Diagram 6-35)*.

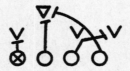

Diagram 6-35

On the split-end side versus a five man front, the double team on the nose guard could be changed so that the offensive guard is blocking the linebackers as part of a double team with the tackle *(Diagram 6-36)*, or the tackle could SUBA *(Diagram 6-37)*. Again, this type of play will be a delay or counter of some type.

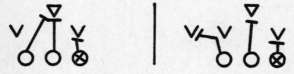

Diagram 6-36   *Diagram 6-37*

7

COACHING THE
MULTIPLE PRO-I
OUTSIDE GAME

Every offense needs outside running plays. The Multiple Pro-I offers four types of sweeps—an outside play with an inside fake (dive option), the option without a dive fake (regular option), a toss sweep (tailback sweep) that gets outside as quickly as possible, and a fourth that takes a little longer to develop but with the blocking patterns provided should bust for the long gain on a high percentage basis (Padre sweep).

COACHING THE OPTIONS

Coaching the Backfield Routes. Our options can be run one of two ways—using the dive option or a regular option. The backfield patterns on the dive option are similar to the dive in that the fullback will dive into the line the same way he would if the fullback dive running play was called. He makes a good fake and expects a hit from the defender in that area *(Diagram 7–1).* The tailback takes his first step slightly back and in the direction of the play, maintaining a good pitch relationship with the quarterback—usually three to five yards in front and five to seven yards behind *(Diagram 7–2).* The tailback will also mirror the quarterback's actions. For instance, if the quarterback goes wide, the tailback also goes wide; if the quarterback cuts up, the tailback cuts up. The tailback must expect the ball to be pitched to him at any time. The quarterback will take the snap, give a good dive fake to the fullback and continue straight down the line of scrimmage looking for the defender, usually the defensive end.

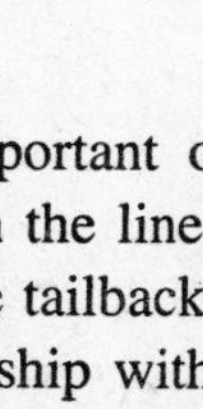

Diagram 7–1 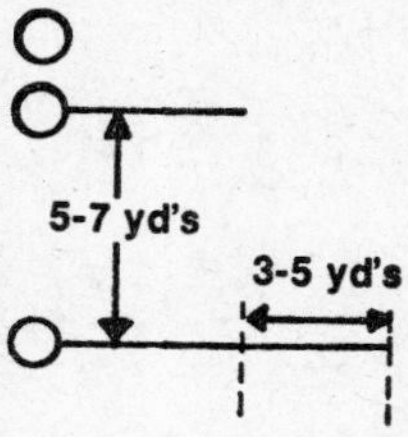   *Diagram 7–2*

It is important on the dive option that the quarterback go straight down the line or into the line, but never away, the reason being that the tailback is forced deeper and usually out of his good pitch relationship with the quarterback. The defense also gains an advantage by having the ball carrier running backward. The correct dive option should have the following characteristics: a good dive fake by the quarterback and fullback, a good straight down the line route by the quarterback, and a tailback maintaining a good pitch position. *(Diagram 7–3)*.

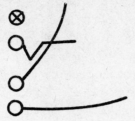

Diagram 7–3

The second option is a type of split-T option where there is no fake into the line. The tailback's responsibility is still the same, and he should always expect the pitch. The quarterback will eliminate the dive fake, but will still come straight down the line with his route. The big change is with the fullback. Instead of faking a dive, he will lead the tailback outside and block the first defender he comes to, usually the defensive cornerback *(Diagram 7–4)*. The tailback must not take off too quickly, it might be added, or the quarterback will not be able to pitch the ball to the tailback because the fullback would be in the way. (This is the reason for the first step being slightly backwards.)

Diagram 7–4

The use of two options enables the coach to take advantage of the big fullback with the dive option. This play will freeze the linebackers and maybe the defensive backs long enough to bust the tailback or quarterbacks free to the outside. The quarterback option will get another blocker in front of the ball carrier.

Both options require a lot of practice time for the quarterback to master the skill of reading the defensive end and to learn to pitch the ball back to the tailback. Our quarterbacks learn to read the belt area of the defender and make their decision off the actions of the defender. If the defender attacks the quarterback, he will pitch the ball immediately to the tailback. If the defender comes across the line of scrimmage and the quarterback cannot see his belt, the best procedure would be for the quarterback to cut upfield and try to break to the outside so that he can still handle the pitch if needed. If the defender sits, the quarterback must run directly at the defender and cause him to make a move. The quarterback will then act accordingly.

The ball is brought to the chest as soon as the quarterback takes the snap or completes his fake, and it should be held there until the pitch. The quarterback will then pitch the ball with one hand closest to the tailback using a shove and a quick outward snap of the wrist. (For example, on an option right, the pitch would be right handed.) If you have the type of quarterback that can run the option, it may be your best play. If your next quarterback is not a good runner, the play may have to be scrapped. Save it for another year.

Coaching the Blocking for Options. The blocking options are broken down into two parts: blocking with the tight end and without a tight end. When blocking without a tight end, the guard and tackle on the play will 3 block and try to turn the defender to the inside.

Diagram 7–5

This block may be easier with the dive fake, and the screen block may be used *(Diagram 7–5)*. The linemen must make sure that meanwhile the defender does not pursue to make the tackle. The split end will block a defensive back depending on the type of secondary the defense is using. The safety will be blocked on a 4-deep *(Diagram 7–6)* while the cornerback will be blocked on a 3-deep *(Diagram 7–7)*. The other lineman will get to the running lane and block the first off color jersey he sees *(Diagram 7–8)*. (The

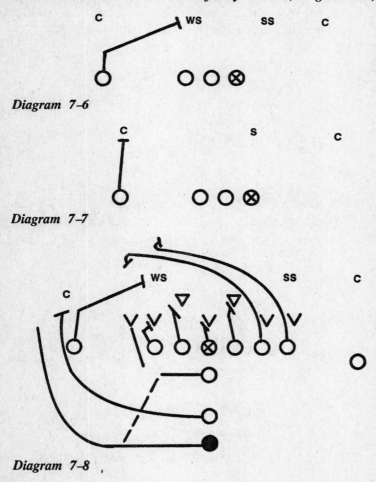

Diagram 7–6

Diagram 7–7

Diagram 7–8

worst the offense can be to the weak side will be when the tailback is one on one with the defensive back, and this will occur when the dive option eliminates the fullback block to the outside.)

The option toward the tight end will be run basically the same way except that we now have an extra blocker in the tight end. The 3 block is still used, but now we do not want to block the defensive end; so we add the word option to our blocking scheme. This tells our tight end to leave the defensive end unblocked so we can option on him. The tight end will therefore release outside of the defensive end and block the first man outside, usually the cornerback *(Diagram 7-9)*.

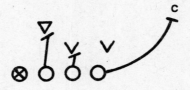

Diagram 7-9

All other blocks stay the same. The flanker will block the safety on the 4-deep secondary and the cornerback on the 3-deep. The offside lineman will get into the running lane and block any off

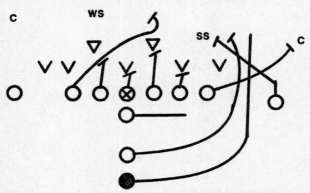

Diagram 7-10   *QB Option Right 3 Option Block*

color jersey. An extra blocker (the fullback) can be picked up by running a quarterback option *(Diagram 7–10)*, while the dive option can be run without any loss of blocking power *(Diagram 7–11)*.

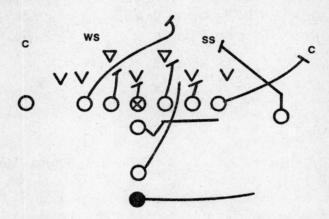

Diagram 7–11   ***Dive Option Right 3 Option Block***

COACHING THE SWEEPS

Coaching the Crack Back Blocks. There is no big secret to coaching the crack back block in the Multiple Pro-I. The only coaching really needed is to make sure the wide receiver is in position to make his block. We try to keep our wide receivers in the same place to eliminate giving away any plays, but if we try to run the sweep toward a defensive end that comes across the line of scrimmage fairly fast, an adjustment has to be made on the split taken by the wide receiver so he can still make the block. We tell our wide receiver to experiment with the defensive ends when they are not too directly involved in a play—that is, a play run away from them or inside. By experimenting they can tell the coach if the sweep can be run or if an off tackle play would be better because the defensive end widens out with them.

As for the block itself, we would like it to be made with the chest and/or shoulders. This means our wide receiver is sitting and waiting for the defender to turn into him. A shoulder block with the head in front of the defender will be made if he is penetrating. This will also be used when blocking downfield—for instance, with the Padre sweep. *(Diagram 7–12)*.

HEAD

Diagram 7–12

Coaching the Down Blocking. The down lineman blocks are the same for the end and tackle as the 0, 1, and 2 blocks. We run two different sweeps, but the same principles are involved. Any time a lineman is to block toward the ball, his main responsibility is to cut off penetration. He does this by stepping directly at the man and driving him down the line of scrimmage with his shoulder. The same holds true if the defender is a lineman or linebacker. The center's block may be one of three. He may use a screen block on a nose guard *(Diagram 7–13)*, a fireout at the linebacker, which can knock him down, screen him, or drive him away from the ball *(Diagram 7–14)*, or a cut block on a defensive lineman on the side of the hole *(Diagram 7–15)*. The techniques used are the same as his regular rules, except for the cut block which is usually made by rolling into the defender after getting the head and shoulders across his front.

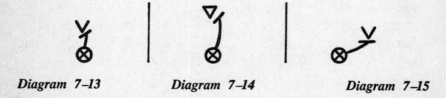

Diagram 7–13   *Diagram 7–14*   *Diagram 7–15*

Coaching the Pulling Guard Routes. The pulling guards are a different area. We spend time before and after practice pulling around bags, goal posts, jerseys or anything else available *(Diagram 7–16)*. To be effective as a pulling guard, depth must be obtained quickly so that the guard can cross the line of scrimmage as close to a ninety degree angle as possible. The lead guard will have more of a bend in his route than the following guard. The elbow being thrown back on the side of the pull helps turn the guard and start his pull correctly. His first step with the lead foot is a turning jab step so the crossover can start getting him depth. Once the correct route is run, repetition is the best way for the guard to get the feel of how deep he must be to run the sweep correctly *(Diagram 7–17)*.

Diagram 7–16

Diagram 7–17

The blocking responsibilities of the trail guard are always the same. The first two or three steps will be straight so as to clear the center and quarterback, then he will bow back to get the required distance to cross the line of scrimmage at a ninety degree angle. Once he gets across the line of scrimmage he will always look to his inside and block an off color jersey *(Diagram 7–18)*.

Diagram 7–18

The lead guard will have two responsibilities, depending on what sweep is called. On a tailback sweep, he will look back inside after turning through the hole. The lead guard on a tailback sweep to the split end side may not pull because of the defense being used *(Diagram 7–19)*. On a Padre sweep, he will block the first man outside, usually the cornerback *(Diagram 7–20)*.

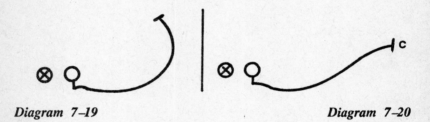

Diagram 7–19   *Diagram 7–20*

Coaching Other Back Blocking Routes. Since the tailback will carry the ball on ninety-nine percent of the sweeps, we will refer to the other back as the fullback. The fullback block will also depend on the type of sweep called. On the tailback sweep, he will lead the tailback outside and block the first defender to appear, usually the cornerback *(Diagram 7–21)*. On the Padre sweep, he must block the man who is playing on the offensive tackle, attack this defender, and not allow any penetration. The path of the lead guard will allow him to go in front and make his block *(Diagram 7–22)*. He must be in position so we line up in a white formation. This gives him the chance to make the block.

Diagram 7-21

Diagram 7-22

SWEEP SYNOPSIS

The two remaining sweeps are shown here *(Diagrams 7-23 & 7-24)* with the tight end and flanker to the right side. This will give a picture of the strongside and weakside play blocking scheme. Since the strongside sweep can be flopped just by putting the tight end to the other side, only one strongside sweep will be shown.

SE—Crack back on defender on the line of scrimmage.

WT—BAS

WG—Will block the linebacker vs. odd front. Either solid or dotted path may be used, whichever is easier. When covered, will down man, BAS.

C—BAS

SG—Pull, use trail guard techniques

ST—Running lane

TE—Running lane

FB—Lead outside

QB—Reverse pivot and give tailback a good "dead" ball on pitch

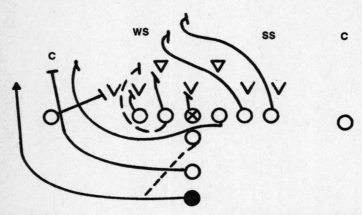

Diagram 7–23   *Tailback Sweep Left (Weakside)*

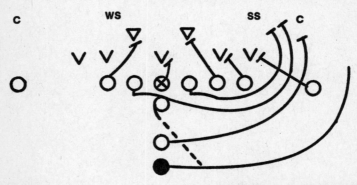

Diagram 7–24   *Tailback Sweep Right (Strongside)*

Fl—Crack back on defender on the line of scrimmage

TE—First man inside, on or off line

ST—First man inside, on or off line

SG—Pull, turn inside

  C—BAS

WG—Pull, trail guard rules

WT—Running lane

FB—Lead tailback outside

QB—Reverse pivot, give tailback "dead" pitch

All rules are the same against even defenses also because of extra blockers in the tight ends. *(Diagram 7–25)*.

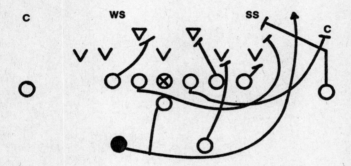

Diagram 7–25   **Padre Sweep Right (Strongside)**

Fl—Downfield, block defensive back according to how many deep there are

TE—BAS; take any way he can but should never allow penetration to the inside. Want play to go outside but will turn inside if defensive end takes hard outside rush or floats outside down line of scrimmage *(Diagrams 7–26 & 7–27)*.

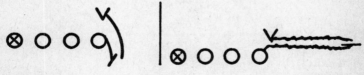

Diagram 7–26   *Diagram 7–27*

ST—First man inside on or off the line of scrimmage

SG—Pull, first man outside; key TE block *(Diagram 7–30)*.

C—BAS

WG—Pull, trail guard rules; key TE block *(Diagram 7–30)*.

WT—Running lane

FB—Block defender on offensive tackle

QB—Get ball to tailback. We prefer handoff on this play.

Could hand off either reverse pivot *(Diagram 7–28)* or open pivot *(Diagram 7–29)*.

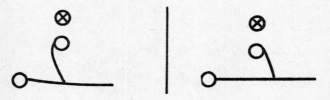

Diagram 7–28   *Diagram 7–29*

TB—QB will get ball to you. Key TE block along with guards. Make a little bend in route so it is easier to key TE block *(Diagram 7–30)*.

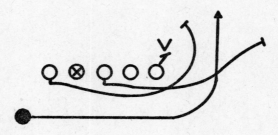

Diagram 7–30

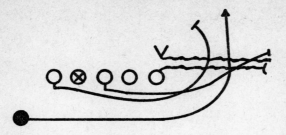

Diagram 7-30 (cont'd.)

SE—Must move inside so as to be able to block the defensive end and not allow any penetration. The rule is basically the same as TE on the other side. If SE is smaller than DE, a screen or cross body block may be used. (If SE cannot handle DE, play should not be used at all.) *(Diagram 7-31.)*

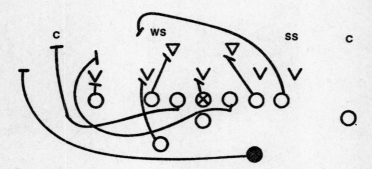

Diagram 7-31   **Padre Sweep Left (Weakside)**

WT—First man inside on or off the line of scrimmage.

WG—Pull, first man outside. Key SE block.

  C—BAS

SG—Pull, trail guards rule. Key SE block.

ST—Running lane

TE—Running lane

FB—Block man on offensive tackle. This blocker could also
   be TB if FB is used to run sweep.

QB—Get ball to TB

TB—Run with ball. Key SE block.

One type of switch block between the tackle and center may be used on an even defense. We work on this block in practice so if the need ever arises in a game situation the linemen can just say "switch" to one another *(Diagram 7–32)*. The center will use a cut block on the defender on the hole side and the tackle will block the linebacker using the BIB technique.

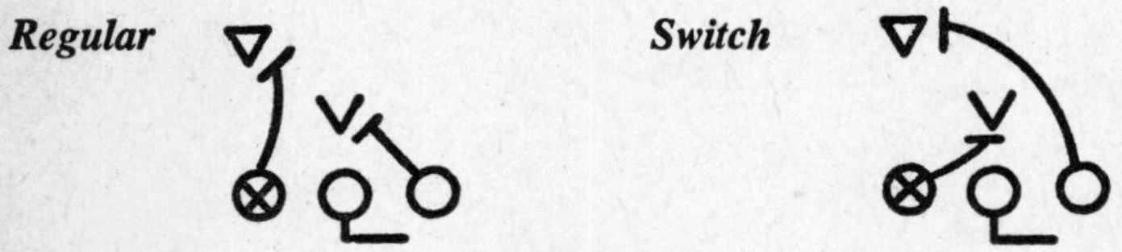

Regular   *Switch*

Diagram 7–32

8

HOW TO COACH THE
ROLL OUT AND
DROP BACK PASSING RULES

The Multiple Pro-I passing game is basically broken down into four different areas: dropbacks, rollouts, play actions, and quicks. We feel that any passing situation that appears in any game could be handled by one or more of these four. Also, we can get any type of action in the backfield or line by using one of the four areas. We divide the passing game into two groups depending on the type of blocking to be used and will discuss first the passive blocking (dropback and rollout), then the aggressive (play action and quick series).

AREA RESPONSIBILITY

On any drop back or roll out blocking pattern we basically block area. This means the linemen, and running backs if necessary, will have a specific area to block. One lineman will be designated as a pivot point for the rest of the blockers to use as a "hinge." On the drop back passes, the pivot man is the center *(Diagram 8–1)*. On the roll out passes, the tackle on the side of the action is the pivot *(Diagrams 8–2 & 8–3)*. The other linemen, knowing this, now can apply their rule of protecting the gap to the inside on any pass (seam blocking). The drop back pass will require that the guards both step sideways to the inside to protect the gap and turn slightly to the outside. The offensive lineman should try to keep the middle open so the quarterback can see—thus the reason for the invitation of the defensive man to the outside.

Diagram 8–1

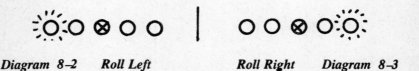

Diagram 8–2   Roll Left   *Roll Right   Diagram 8–3*

The tackles will step inside to protect the inside seam on this play while stepping backward and turning slightly outside, once again inviting the defender to take the outside pass rush. This position beside the guard should be one yard deeper than the guard, giving the offensive line a "cup" protection look. The tackles should invite the defense more to the outside than the offensive guards do. This will give the quarterback the line of sight needed and a possible running lane up the middle when necessary.

Regardless of the formation used, the backs will divide block with the fullback going to the side of the two receivers most of the time. Each will take the area immediately outside of the tackle on their side. They too will invite the defensive man to the outside so that their block will be a "ride" block taking the defender around and behind the quarterback. This block is made by putting the head on the outside of the defender and riding him back and out, using the shoulder.

The complete drop back blocking will then form a cup and should look like *Diagram 8–4*. The line should give enough ground on the snap so that the center is one to two yards off the ball and the cup forms around him. The quarterback will set at eight to ten yards and deliver the ball from six to eight yards.

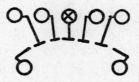

Diagram 8–4

This type of drop back protection is ideal against any type of defense, whether reading or stunting. The main coaching point here is to close off the inside gaps. A typical stunt from a five man front versus the drop back cup may look like *Diagram 8–5*. *Note:* The linebackers are picked up as well as the slanting nose guard. The defensive ends have a long way to go, and this hopefully will give the quarterback time to deliver the ball.

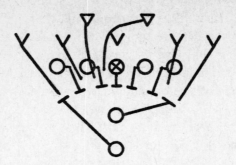

Diagram 8-5

The blocking for the roll out passes have the same rules but a different pivot man. Also, the fullback now must go in the direction of the call and block the first man outside of the pivot man. The block away from the pivot is a step to close the gaps and a retreat to form a lopsided cup. The tailback may help on the weak side or release for a pass. The quarterback will set up basically from eight to ten yards deep behind the pivot man. Hitting a shorter pattern will cut down quarterback set up yardage and time used in throwing but not the lineman blocking patterns. Roll right blocking will look like *Diagram 8-6*. (We would like to hook the defensive end with the fullback, but this is not something the fullback must do.) A roll left blocking pattern would look like *Diagram 8-7*.

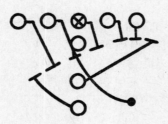

Diagram 8-6

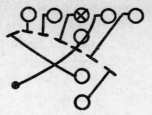

Diagram 8–7

Any stunt that goes away from the direction of the roll is ignored until the defender threatens the protection cup forming around the quarterback *(Diagram 8–8)*. Any defense that runs a stunt into our roll out pass should be blocked without any trouble or change of assignments *(Diagram 8–9)*.

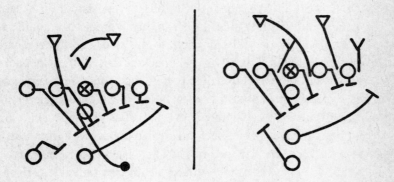

Diagram 8–8   *Diagram 8–9*

We are very confident of our pass protection. Over the past four years, we have averaged fifteen pass attempts a game with less than two quarterback sacks. We have had two quarterbacks who each passed for over 1,200 yards in a single season and completed slightly over fifty percent of their passes while throwing a total of 32 passes between them.

THE BLITZING LINEBACKER

With our pass blocking rules, we really don't worry too much about blitzing linebackers because gaps are covered and this is the usual route of the linebackers. We warn our free linemen, however, always to be on the lookout for them because the linebacker can get to the gap faster than a lineman, especially if the linebacker is guessing the snap count. Our rule, therefore, is to check the gap inside for any blitzing but be able to help out inside or out if the linebacker doesn't appear. This type of blocking eliminates the guard being responsible for a linebacker going around the other side of the nose guard and being cut off by the center.

ALTERNATE RESPONSIBILITIES

Our so-called alternate responsibilities consist of just being able to help out to either side. If a team has a great nose guard, we will tell our center he will have help to the side with either guard. The guard still must check the linebacker, but if the linebacker doesn't appear, he will automatically help the center. The same goes for the tackle, especially on a pass called in his direction. In this case, the fullback can also help if his man does not appear. On any roll out pass, the weakside lineman can also break away from a strict gap rule to pick up any defender. This can happen any time a linebacker does not blitz and will also enable the tailback to release on a pattern *(Diagram 8–10)*. In *Diagram 8–10* the nose guard is blocked by the center. The weak guard steps to the inside gap and checks for the linebacker. If the linebacker is going back, he will tell the tackle (who has also stepped to his gap and is started back) and will block A or B automatically. The tailback, meanwhile, has set up outside the tackle, hears and sees what is going on, and releases to the outside and looks for an open area while yelling a code word to the quarterback meaning he has released. If at any time the fullback's man doesn't appear and he has nobody to block, he also will release, yelling the code word. Both backs are taught to raise their hands while yelling so the quarterback can see them. The coaches during the practice week will tell the running backs and quarterbacks what short areas should be open. This type of pattern could be called "hot" and could be the code word yelled by the running back when he releases.

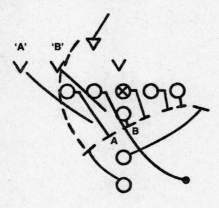

Diagram 8–10

9

MULTIPLE PRO-I
PLAY ACTION PASS
BLOCKING RULES

Every offense has its play action passes, their purpose being mainly to pass the ball while having the play look like a run. The Pro-I is no different. The play action passes used in the Pro-I will depend on what type of running plays are being used with success in any particular season. One year, for instance, we had a quick fullback who ran a dive very well and a good tailback with excellent speed outside. We sent them one way on a dive option fake, brought the quarterback away from them, and threw deep to the split end.

This play alone was responsible for eight touchdown passes in one season. The next year, not one touchdown pass came on this play because our offensive running game had taken on a different look. Our tailback this particular year was more of a slashing runner who ran well between the tackles. One play action pass off an inside running fake was responsible for five touchdown passes to the tight end and numerous other long gains. The flanker in the same year had a total of ten touchdown catches as a result of additional play action passes. The point here is that the play action pass is only as good as your running attack. If you have one, two, or three good receivers and a quarterback that can get the ball to them, the play action series may not be for you. The roll out or drop back might be best. If you do have a running attack and the receivers to go with it, you could almost drive an opponent off the field using the play action pass and the Pro-I offense.

LINEMEN

On a play action pass, the offensive linemen must be aggressive on the play fake side and passive on the weak side. The aggressive linemen must attack the defense as if it were a running play. The head should go on the same side of the defender on which the quarterback will be setting up. Practice time in drilling, where the quarterback will set up, will help the linemen know which side the quarterback will be throwing from *(Diagram 9–1)*.

Diagram 9–1

On the play fake side, if a linebacker is lined up on an offensive lineman, the location of the linebacker will usually determine the lineman's block. If the linebacker blitzes, the lineman will block him *(Diagram 9–2)*. If the linebacker retreats for a pass, the lineman will step up and over to his gap in the direction of the play and help the man to either side *(Diagram 9–3)*.

Diagram 9–2   Diagram 9–3

If the lineman can reach the linebacker on his initial charge, he will fire out aggressively, giving an indication of a running play in his direction *(Diagram 9–4)*. The center will use the same technique involved in roll out protection if he is free *(Diagram 9–5)*. If he is covered, he will fire out, making contact, then step back, turning the defender away from the play *(Diagram 9–6)*.

Diagram 9–4   Diagram 9–5

Diagram 9–6

The weakside linemen will be a little passive but back far enough to block a defender who is taking an outside pass rush. The guard's duties, if he is covered, are the same as the rollout except that he will not pull back as far *(Diagram 9–7)*. If he has a linebacker on him, he must take one good step forward to freeze the linebacker, then retreat *(Diagram 9–8)*. The tackle is passive as with the rollout except that the depth coming back is not the same. It is a little shallower *(Diagram 9–9)*.

Diagram 9–7    *Diagram 9–8*    *Diagram 9–9*

BACKFIELD RESPONSIBILITIES

The backfield assignments are fairly easy, the only real task being to carry out the running play fake. This means not only going to the correct area but also accepting the fake and going through with more than one step in the direction of the backfield flow. In most cases, the running back faked to should be tackled or bumped if he is doing his job correctly and can very easily fill in for a pulling lineman *(Diagram 9–10)*. If one back is blocking, the other back is usually in some type of pass pattern—either a called pattern or a hot one (discussed in Chapter 8).

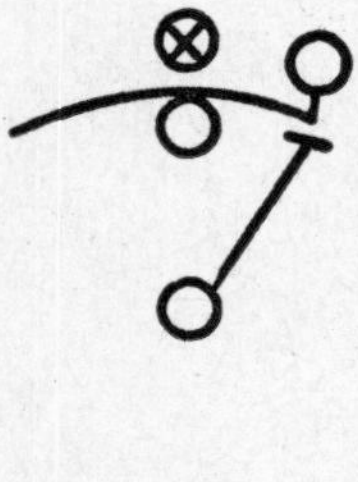

Diagram 9–10

QUICK PASSING GAME

In the Pro-I, the quick passing series is included in the play action passes because of the blocking of the line. The quicks are just exactly that, quick passes thrown from a depth of one to two yards. The linemen blocks are aggressive all up and down the line. The offensive linemen will fire out at the defender's knees to make the defender stay low. This gives the quarterback better vision to see his receivers. The linemen do not have to maintain the block because the ball will be thrown very quickly but it is imperative that contact is made with the defender. If a linebacker is on an offensive lineman and can be reached with a long fire out block, the lineman will do so *(Diagram 9–11)*. If the linebacker is so deep he cannot be reached, the offensive lineman will then help his teammate to either side depending on which one needs it the most *(Diagram 9–12)*. (This will be discussed during the week of practice.)

Diagram 9–11

Diagram 9–12

On the quick series, the backs could have a variety of things to do. One of the first is blocking either inside or out depending on what the coaching staff prefers. Blocking inside would be helping out on blitzing linebackers or penetrating linemen *(Diagram 9–13)*; outside would mean blocking the defensive end *(Diagram 9–14)*.

(Remember, this is a quick passing series; so the blocks from the backs must be of a very aggressive nature.)

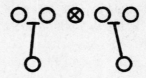

Diagram 9–13

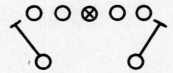

Diagram 9–14

The backs may also be used as a safety valve pass pattern in case the other receivers are covered. The pattern we run is called a flare *(Diagram 9–15)*. Each back goes in a different direction at full speed and looks over his inside shoulder. The pattern must be run fast enough to get outside of the defensive ends.

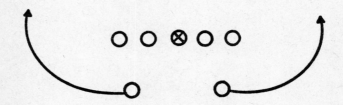

Diagram 9–15

PULLING GUARDS

Some of the play action passes in the Pro-I do have the need for a pulling guard. In the Pro-I, the guards run the same route whether it is a pass or run. This way the guard is not confused with two different pulling routes. He knows that if he pulls right he will pull right the same way all the time. The only thing he must remember is not to cross the line of scrimmage on a pass.

The guard's responsibility is usually the defensive end no matter what type of defense we are playing against. The charge of the defensive end will determine how the guard will block him (that is, hook, ride outside, or almost no block at all.) The guard's normal route is just like his running play route *(Diagram 9–16)*.

Diagram 9–16

As we all know, however, it is not always that easy. As the guard is clearing the center he will be able to adjust his route to whatever the defensive end is doing. If the end comes across hard, the guard must ride him to the outside and let the quarterback stop and set up *(Diagram 9–17)*. If the end sits, the guard may be able to hook him inside and let the quarterback get outside *(Diagram 9–18)*. If the end goes inside or retreats for a pass protection, the guard will come outside and listen for the word "go" from the quarterback which indicates that the quarterback is going to run the ball *(Diagram 9–19)*.

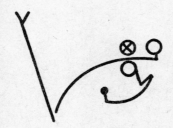

Diagram 9–17

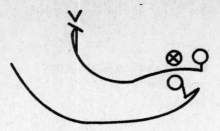

Diagram 9–18

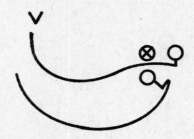

Diagram 9–19

   If two guards are pulling, the second one will be used as a "clean-up" man, that is blocking anybody who happens to break through the blocks at the line of scrimmage. Very seldom would both guards be pulled on the same play. Keeping the near side guard in gives a better seal to the play side.

10

HOW TO CAPITALIZE
ON PASS PATTERNS

As mentioned earlier, the pass patterns in the Pro-I are given a number which is correlated for all three receivers. If we want a receiver to run a specific pattern, we can still call it. At the beginning of the year, we teach a passing tree to all receivers. Once the tree is being run and has been learned, we start giving the patterns numbers—numbers which evolve into patterns if based on complimentary routes, making it easier to call in the huddle. For example, a flanker running a curl, a tight end running a swing and up and a split end running a post pattern would more easily be referred to as a "4 pattern." In the description of the tree given below, we will explain how we number our passing game and how the pattern is usually called for each receiver. In all cases, every pass pattern could be called immediately.

INDIVIDUAL PASS PATTERNS

Split End

The split end passing tree will be drawn up from the left. Very seldom does our split end go right. His tree is shown in *Diagram 10–1*.

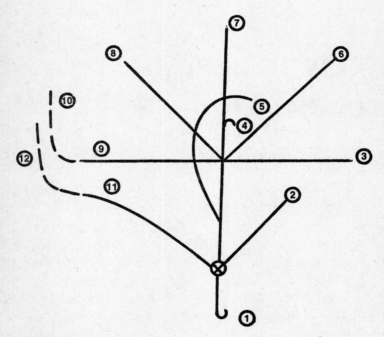

Diagram 10–1

1. Hitch—At the snap, the split end will take one or two steps backward and receive the ball looking directly at the quarterback. The pattern is usually run from a quick series and will seldom have any blocking. Blocking for this play can come from a lineman who will sprint to get in front of the wide receiver and block the first defender in that area *(Diagram 10–2)*.

Diagram 10–2

2. Look-in—The look-in is a quick pattern run at a 45° angle to the inside. The ball should be received at a depth of five to seven yards from the inside. This pattern is run from the quick series and is an ideal pass from the audible system because of this quickness *(Diagram 10–3)*.

Diagram 10–3

3. Drag—The drag pattern will be used to bring the split end completely across the defensive formation. The pattern itself is set up by going straight upfield for five yards then breaking to the inside, going across the defensive formation either in front or behind the linebackers. The exact depth of this pattern will be determined by how the linebackers are playing the pass. If the linebackers are dropping deep, the pattern will be run in front of or under them; if the linebackers are shallow, the drag will be run behind them. This pattern is part of the 3 pattern *(Diagram 10–4)*.

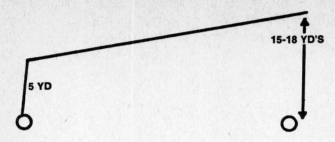

15-18 YD'S

5 YD

Diagram 10-4

4. Hook—We usually use this pattern when we are looking for a first down. The receiver must know how much yardage is needed and run his pattern accordingly, two or three yards more than is necessary so he can come back to the ball if need be. The split end will hook to his inside and be looking directly back at the quarterback. The hook pattern is part of our 1 and 9 patterns *(Diagram 10-5).*

Diagram 10-5

5. Curl—Over the years, this pattern has been our most consistent for the split end. He will go straight upfield for about five yards then break slightly outside and make a bend to the inside. How far inside the receiver will curl will depend on the linebacker's drop zone. If the linebacker goes more outside in his drop zone, the pattern will be run to the inside. If the linebacker's drop is straight back, the receiver will curl to his outside. The split end should be fifteen to seventeen yards deep, facing the quarterback so that he can see the number on his chest. The curl is part of the 6 pattern *(Diagram 10–6)*.

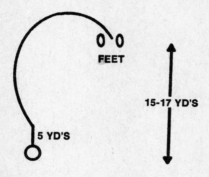

Diagram 10–6

6. Post—This pattern is a deep route which is run directly at the goal post. The receivers will run five to ten yards before breaking toward the post, depending on how the defense is playing him. The ball will be received over the inside shoulder. The post is part of the 2 pattern and the GOB left *(Diagram 10–7)*.

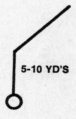

Diagram 10–7

7. Fly—This pattern will take advantage of the straight away speed of the split end. No fakes or turns are involved, and the ball will be received over the inside shoulder *(Diagram 10–8)*.

Diagram 10–8

8. Flag—The flag is another deep pattern run to the flags in the corner of the end zone. There are two types of flag patterns in the Pro-I. The regular pattern is a straight one, five to ten yards, then to the flag *(Diagram 10–9)*. The other is where the receiver comes at an angle as if to block a defensive back and then turns out to the flag *(Diagram 10–10)*. The latter pattern is called the action flag and is used on play action fakes; the regular flag is part of the 7 pattern. The action flag is part of the 8 pattern, flood left and GOB right. The ball is received over the outside shoulder in either of the patterns.

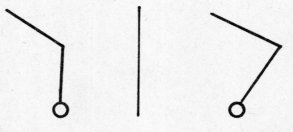

Diagram 10–9   *Diagram 10–10*

9. Out—This pattern is designed to look like a deep pattern and then go medium to the outside. The break will come at ten to fifteen yards depending on the defense *(Diagram 10–11)*. The ball is received over the outside shoulder, and the pattern may also be bent back to the quarterback if the need arises *(Diagram 10–12)*. This pattern may be good to get first down yardage. The bending back toward the quarterback is a good protection pass against a defensive back who is covering the receiver well. The receiver must go beyond the yardage needed for the first down so that when the ball is caught he will have the necessary yardage.

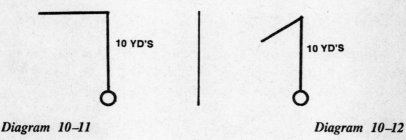

Diagram 10–11   *Diagram 10–12*

10. Out and Up—The out and up pattern is designed to take advantage of an overly aggressive defensive back who is playing the receiver tight to make the tackle on the out pattern or hoping for an

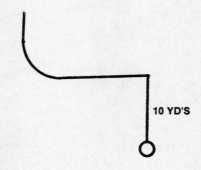

Diagram 10–13

interception. The ball will be delivered over the inside shoulder as the receiver turns upfield. The ball should be thrown high enough to clear the defensive back *(Diagram 10–13)*.

11. Swing—The swing is a quick hitting pattern to the outside and is part of the quick series. The release on this pattern should be at a 45° angle to the outside and run five to ten yards deep. The ball is thrown over the outside shoulder *(Diagram 10–14)*.

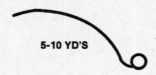

5-10 YD'S

Diagram 10–14

12. Swing and Up—Again, the swing and up is designed to take advantage of the aggressive defensive back. Since it is part of the quick series, the ball will be delivered very quickly for a "deep pattern" and will be received over the inside shoulder probably no deeper than fifteen to twenty yards. The ball must be thrown over the defensive back *(Diagram 10–15)*.

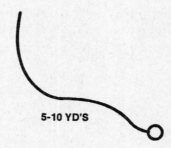

5-10 YD'S

Diagram 10–15

Tight End

All patterns for the tight end will be drawn from a right formation. If the tight end is to go left, his numbered patterns will be the same as the flanker when the flanker appears on the left side *(Diagram 10–16)*.

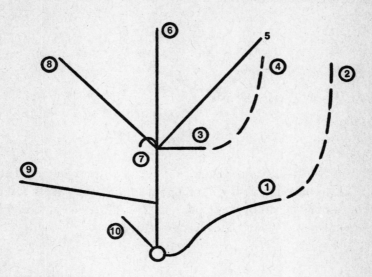

Diagram 10–16

1. Swing—The swing is a quick hitting pattern to the outside. The release should be at a 45° angle with the break coming at five to ten yards deep. The ball is received over the outside shoulder. The swing is part of the 2 pattern and GOB left *(Diagram 10–17)*.

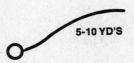

5-10 YD'S

Diagram 10–17

2. Swing and Up—The swing and up is run with the tight end mainly as part of the 4 pattern to put pressure on the defensive back.

It could also be used as a pattern to take advantage of the tight end's speed and/or an overly aggressive back. The ball is received over the inside shoulder *(Diagram 10–18)*.

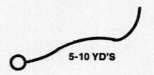

Diagram 10–18

3. **Out**—The out pattern is run ten to fifteen yards and at a 90° break to the outside. It will compliment the deep pattern run by the flanker and is part of the flood right series. The ball is received over the outside shoulder *(Diagram 10–19)*.

Diagram 10–19

4. **Out and Up**—This pattern is the same as the out pattern with a turn upfield to take advantage of the speed or inside move of the flanker. The ball is received over the inside shoulder *(Diagram 10–20)*.

5. **Flag**—The flag pattern is run five to ten yards straight upfield and breaks to the flag in the corner of the end zone. The ball is delivered over the outside shoulder *(Diagram 10–21)*.

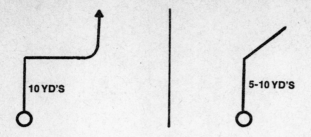

Diagram 10-20   *Diagram 10-21*

6. Fly—The fly pattern is run straight up with no fakes or angles and is used to take advantage of the speed of the tight end. The ball is received over the inside shoulder *(Diagram 10-22)*.

7. Hook—This pattern is designed to go straight upfield for two or three yards past the first down yardage. The tight end will hook inside so the quarterback can see the numbers. The hook is part of the 1 and 9 patterns *(Diagram 10-23)*.

Diagram 10-22   *Diagram 10-23*

8. Post—The post pattern should run five to ten yards straight upfield, then break in toward the goal post. The ball is thrown over the inside shoulder. The post is part of the 3, 6 and 8 patterns *(Diagram 10-24)*.

Diagram 10–24

9. Drag—The tight end will run the drag pattern across the defense after making his initial break at three to four yards. The depth of the drag pattern will depend on the drops of the linebackers. If the linebackers drop deep, the tight end will come under them. If the linebackers play close to the line of scrimmage, the pattern will go behind them. We want this pattern to be run under (in front of) the linebacker ninety-nine percent of the time. It is part of the 7 and GOB right patterns *(Diagram 10–25)*.

10. Look-in—The look-in is a part of the quick series, and it is especially good against blitzing linebackers. The ball is received over the inside shoulder of the quarterback *(Diagram 10–26)*.

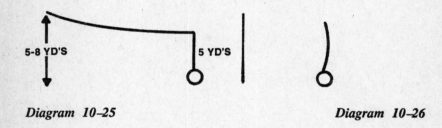

Diagram 10–25   *Diagram 10–26*

Flanker

The flanker will have two sets of patterns—one from his regular set and one from the slot. Two different trees will be drawn so the different patterns can be seen from the two formations *(Diagrams 10–27 & 10–41)*.

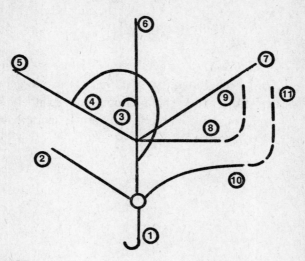

Diagram 10–27

1. Hitch—The flanker will take one or two steps backward on the hitch and face the quarterback to receive the ball. This pattern is used to take advantage of the quickness of the receiver and is part of the quick series *(Diagram 10–28)*.

FEET

Diagram 10–28

2. Look-in—The flanker will release inside at a 45° angle on the look-in and will receive the ball from the inside. The look-in is part of the quick series and is used when the defensive back is playing to his outside *(Diagram 10–29)*.

Diagram 10–29

3. Hook—The hook is a good pass to use to get a first down and should be run two to three yards past the yardage needed. The flanker will hook inside and look back at the quarterback. The hook is part of the 1 pattern *(Diagram 10–30)*.

Diagram 10–30

4. Curl—The curl pattern is the flanker's most important pattern because it consistently yields good yardage and is a high percentage completion pass. The flanker on the curl will release straight for five yards, then bend to the outside and back inside to the necessary depth of fifteen to seventeen yards. The flanker and the quarterback should be reading the same linebacker; so the location where the ball will be caught will depend on the linebacker. If the linebacker's drop zone is outside, the flanker will curl around him to the inside to receive the ball. If the linebacker drops straight back to the inside, the flanker will receive the ball to the linebacker's outside. The receiver should be turned so that the quarterback can see the number on his jersey. The curl is part of the 4 pattern *(Diagram 10–31)*.

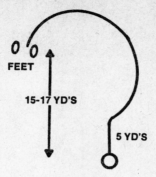

Diagram 10-31

5. Post—The flanker will run straight for five to ten yards and break inside, going for the goal post. The post is a speed pattern for the flanker, and the ball will be received over the inside shoulder. The post is part of the GOB right pattern *(Diagram 10-32)*.

6. Fly—The fly is strictly a speed pattern. The ball will be delivered over the inside shoulder and the pattern is run as straight upfield as possible *(Diagram 10-33)*.

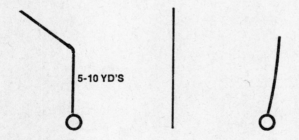

Diagram 10-32   *Diagram 10-33*

7. Flag—This pattern is another deep route for the flanker. It is run two different ways like the split end flag pattern. The regular pattern is straight up for five to ten yards, then out to the goal line flags. The action flag requires a pattern inside so as to block the

defensive back and then outside to the flag. The pattern must not be
run so far inside as to prevent a good route from being run. In both
patterns, the ball is received over the outside shoulder and they are
part of the 2, 3 and GOB left flood right patterns *(Diagrams 10–34
& 10–35).*

Diagram 10–34   *Diagram 10–35*

8. Out—The out pattern is a ten to fifteen yard pattern used
when the defensive back is playing off the receiver. The ball is
received to the outside and the pass route may be bent back if
needed *(Diagrams 10–36 & 10–37).*

Diagram 10–36   *Diagram 10–37*

9. Out and Up—This pattern is used to take advantage of an
aggressive defensive back who is trying for the interception. The
pattern is the same as the out except that the quarterback fakes and

throws the ball over the defensive back to the inside shoulder of the receiver *(Diagram 10–38)*.

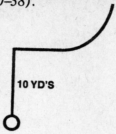

Diagram 10–38

10. Swing—The swing is part of the quick series, and is a five to ten yard pattern. The ball is thrown a lot sooner than the out pattern and is received over the outside shoulder. This pattern is good when the defensive back is playing tight and to the receiver's inside *(Diagram 10–39)*.

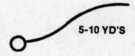

Diagram 10–39

11. Swing and Up—The swing and up is another pattern to take advantage of an aggressive defensive back. The ball will be thrown high enough to clear the defender as soon as the receiver makes his turn upfield. This pattern is part of the quick series *(Diagram 10–40)*.

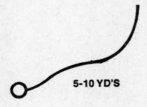

Diagram 10–40

The flanker's other position is the slot. The patterns he will run from that formation are shown in *Diagram 10–41*.

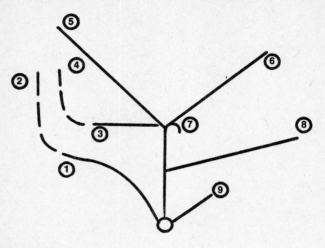

Diagram 10–41

1. **Swing**—The swing pattern here is the same as the swing on the other side and is part of the 8 pattern *(Diagram 10–42)*.

2. **Swing and Up**—This pattern, too, is the same as on the other side and is used to put pressure on a defensive back as part of the 6 pattern *(Diagram 10–43)*.

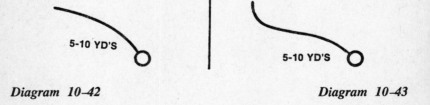

Diagram 10–42   *Diagram 10–43*

3. **Out**—The out pattern is the same as the other side and is part of the flood left series *(Diagram 10–44)*.

Diagram 10-44

4. Out and Up—This pattern is the same *(Diagram 10-45)*.

5. Flag—The flag pattern from this position will be run the regular way. The flag will be called for the flanker to run this as it is not part of the numbered patterns of the Pro-I *(Diagram 10-46)*.

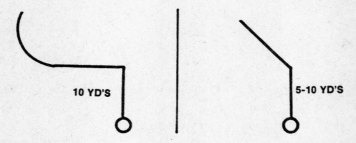

Diagram 10-45   *Diagram 10-46*

6. Post—The post is the same here as the other side and is part of the 7 pattern *(Diagram 10-47)*.

7. Hook—The hook is also the same but is part of the 9 pattern *(Diagram 10-48)*.

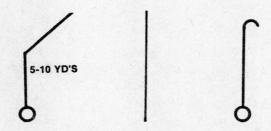

Diagram 10-47   *Diagram 10-48*

8. Deep drag—The deep drag will be run behind the linebacker to a point fifteen to eighteen yards off the line of scrimmage. The pass pattern is used on the play fake away from the direction of the pattern and is commonly used on the GOB left pass *(Diagram 10–49)*.

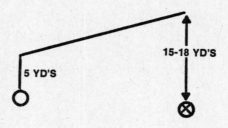

Diagram 10–49

9. Look-in—The look-in is not used much from this formation because too many defensive men could be in the catch area. It is part of the quick series *(Diagram 10–50)*.

Diagram 10–50

Tailback

The tailback has three basic patterns. To make things easier in the huddle, we also put a letter identification on some of these patterns. For example, an "A" or a "D" would be connected with the flare pattern depending on which direction the tailback is to go. The letters "B" and "C" refer to the seam pattern and are used to indicate the direction of the tailback *(Diagram 10–51)*.

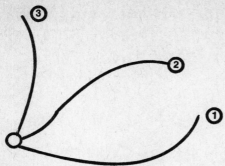

Diagram 10–51

1. **Flare**—The first two steps of the flare must be back and in the direction of the flow. How fast the pattern will be run will depend on the play and the defense. If the tailback is the primary receiver, the pattern must be run quickly. If the tailback is the secondary receiver, then the route would depend on how the defense is playing him. The ball is received over the inside shoulder. The letter "A" here would indicate a flare pattern in the direction of the flow while a "D" would indicate a flare pattern away from the flow *(Diagram 10–51)*.

2. **Swing**—The swing is a five yard pattern which must be run hard to get out of the backfield in time to be effective. The ball is received over the outside shoulder. The swing is part of the flood pattern *(Diagram 10–51)*.

3. **Seam**—The seam pattern is run between the linemen. The tailback must be careful not to get held up by the defensive linemen. The seam is usually a good delay type of pattern. The ball is received over the inside shoulder. The letter "B" would indicate a seam pattern in the direction of the flow, while a "C" indicates a seam pattern run away from the flow *(Diagram 10–51)*.

Fullback

The fullback, not being a primary pass receiver, is limited to two basic patterns. The seam pattern is more of a safety valve pass for him, whereas the swing pass is the only pattern in which he is the primary receiver *(Diagram 10–52)*.

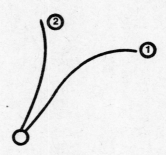

Diagram 10–52

   1. Swing—The swing pattern for the fullback is the same as for the tailback and is used as part of the slant passes *(Diagram 10–52)*.

   2. Seam—The seam pattern for the fullback is also the same as the tailback and is part of the GOB patterns *(Diagram 10–52)*.

COACHING THE NUMBERED ROUTES

   In devising the numbering system to be used in the Pro-I offense, consideration was given to the type of patterns that would compliment each other. We also thought about where we wanted these key patterns to be run, how deep the pattern should be run, in what direction the receivers should be moving, and how deep the quarterback would be setting up.

   We started with the quarterback and the primary receiver on each pattern. We figured that the quarterback should be able to set up at eight to ten yards for every main receiver. If a quicker opening pattern was desired, the quarterback could set up more quickly. As the quarterback comes back from the line of scrimmage, he is looking at the quick receiver; and if he is open, the quarterback will deliver the ball. If the quick receiver is not open, the quarterback will continue back to where he should set up and look for his primary target. We want the ball thrown to the primary receiver but not if the quarterback has to "force" the ball into him.

In some patterns all receivers will be open at the same time, and the quarterback will have to read a defender to decide who to throw the ball to. Other patterns will have the three receivers open at different times; so if one is not open, the quarterback can look elsewhere for the next receiver. We have the receivers in the same area of sight for the quarterback, only at different depths.

The next thing considered was the direction of the roll and where to position the flanker. It was decided that the numbers 1 through 4 would mean that the flanker lines up normally. The line knows then that a roll 1, roll 2, etc. means the quarterback is rolling right; so the roll right protection is used. If a dropback 1, dropback 2, etc. is called, the line would use dropback protection, and the flanker would still go to the right side. The numbers 6 through 9 mean that the flanker will line up in the slot; so the side of two receivers is now to the left. The roll 6, roll 7, etc. call will tell the lineman a roll left protection will be used, while a dropback 6 will get dropback protection. All roll out patterns will roll in the direction of the two receivers.

Next, the patterns to be used were determined. It was decided that if the pattern was good to one side it had to be good to the other, so a mirrored effect came about.

With all of this in mind then, the numbered patterns are those shown in *Diagrams 10–53 to 10–60*. All receivers will hook to the inside on the 1 and 9 patterns. If the first down yardage is required, all receivers should know how many yards are needed and run their patterns accordingly.

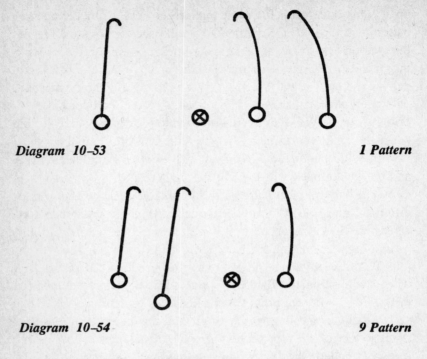

Diagram 10–53   *1 Pattern*

Diagram 10–54   *9 Pattern*

All three receivers will break at the same time. The quarterback must read the linebacker to decide which one to throw to.

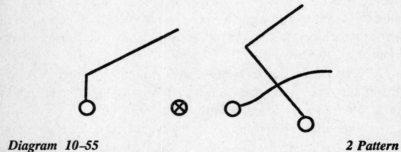

Diagram 10–55   *2 Pattern*

SE—Post

TE—Swing. The tight end is the quick receiver running a 5-10 pattern. If he runs into the sideline, he will automatically run the swing and up pattern.

Fl—Action flag. The inside move will depend on the speed of the flanker and the opponent's defense.

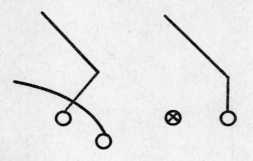

Diagram 10–56 **8 Pattern**

SE—Action flag
Fl—Swing
TE—Post

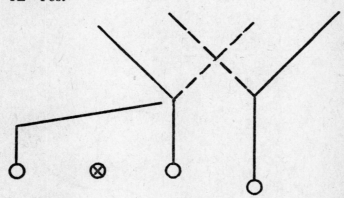

Diagram 10–57 **3 Pattern**

SE—Drag pattern—The depth will depend on the linebackers,

and the ball may be delivered any time after the SE passes the center's position.

TE—Post } The ball will be thrown to either, if open.

Fl—Flag } They can also switch patterns in which a 3 switch is called in the dotted lines. The outside receiver will always go first.

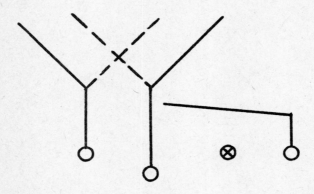

Diagram 10–58   **7 Pattern**

SE—Flag. }
Fl—Post } 7, switch (dotted lines)
TE—Drag

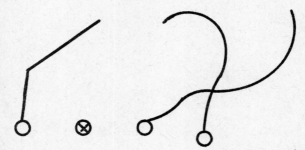

Diagram 10–59   **4 Pattern**

SE—Post

TE—Swing and up. This is designed to put pressure on the defensive back who cheats inside to help out the flanker.

Fl—Curl

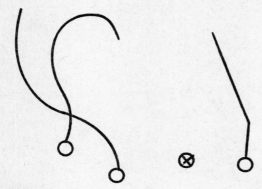

Diagram 10–60   *6 Pattern*

SE—Curl

Fl—Swing and up

TE—Post

PLAY ACTION PATTERNS

The patterns used with the play action passes in the Pro-I are standardized. This does not mean they cannot be changed; they can be by calling a different pattern in the huddle. We try to keep the patterns the same to eliminate confusion and keep down the time spent in the huddle.

The patterns *(Diagrams 10–61 to 10–69)* are no different from those discussed on the passing tree. The action flag pattern is now used to simulate the blocking angle instead of the regular route. The play action passes are broken down into GOB's, slip passes, slant passes, quicks, floods, and sweep passes. The pass from a dive fake could be either a GOB or a quick, depending on what type of pattern or play fake is needed. (The quick pattern will not be discussed here but will be included in the next chapter when all phases are put together.) Running backs will line up in a position where it is easier for them to get into the pattern.

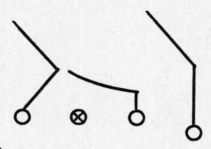

Diagram 10-61   **GOB Right**

SE—Action flag
TE—Drag
Fl—Post

GOB

The GOB is a pass which means guard opposite backs. It is run off a dive fake. Patterns will depend on the formation and the right or left call *(Diagrams 10-61 & 10-62)*.

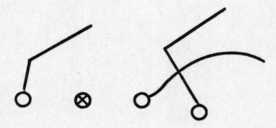

Diagram 10-62   **GOB Left**

SE—Post
TE—Swing
Fl—Action flag

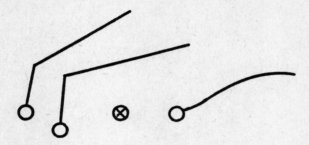

Diagram 10-63   *Slot, GOB Left*

SE—Post
Fl—Deep drag
TE—Swing

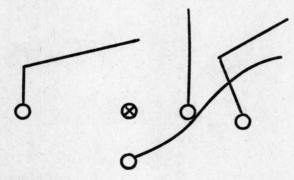

Diagram 10-64   *Slant, Pass Right*

SE—Drag

TE—Fly

Fl—Action flag

FB—Swing

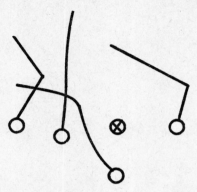

Diagram 10-65   **Slot, Slant Pass Left**

SE—Action flag

Fl—Fly

TE—Drag

FB—Swing

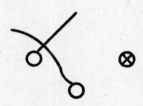

Diagram 10-66   **Slip Pass Left**

SE—Look-in; fly

TB—Swing

Other—Any pattern as long as they stay out of the tailback's
area.

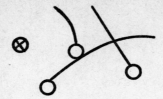

Diagram 10–67   *Slip Pass Right*

    TE—Look-in
    Fl—Look-in
    TB—Swing

FLOODS

We classify the flood pattern as a play action because it can be run similar to the slip pass by faking to the fullback. Basically, it is a roll out pass—but with three receivers flooding one side of the field. *(Diagrams 10–68 & 10–69)*.

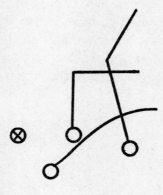

Diagram 10–68   *Flood Right*

SE—Post
TE—Out
Fl—Action flag
TB—Swing

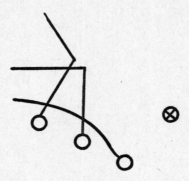

Diagram 10–69   **Flood Left**

SE—Action flag
Fl—Out
TB—Swing
TE—Post

These play action passes are just some of the set pattern plays in the Pro-I. Any pattern can be changed to meet any pattern on the tree—or made up to take advantage of any defensive situation that may arise. To take advantage of a play that was not discussed here, the word "pass" can be added along with a pattern, and a new play is born.

11

ROLLS AND QUICKS

The passing game for the Pro-I can be put together in pieces. Usually, the line will be separated from the backs and ends so that each area can get as much work in as possible. At all times, the line should be reminded where the passer will be throwing, and the passer should be reminded where his blocking help is going to be. When the two areas are brought together, then, the mesh should be quite smooth. Practice time will insure this smoothness; in fact the passing game should be practiced so much, that throwing from the end zone on a first or second down becomes second nature.

ROLLS

As was mentioned in Chapter 10, our numbered patterns are the same, regardless of whether we roll out or drop back. We roll in the Pro-I because hard pressure is usually exerted only on one side. It also gives our quarterback a chance to get outside and run if necessary. The curl patterns to each side (4 and 6) are the most important, and, accordingly, we spend more time on this type of pattern in practice. Some examples of our roll out game are roll 4-A *(Diagram 11–1)*, roll 3-C *(Diagram 11–2)*, roll 2-B *(Diagram 11–3)*, roll 6-A *(Diagram 11–4)*, roll 9-D *(Diagram 11–5)*, and dropback 7-C *(Diagram 11–6)*.

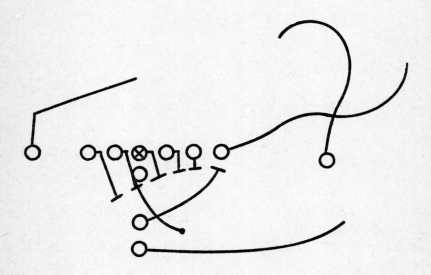

Diagram 11–1   **Roll 4-A**

The quarterback on the roll 4-A will set at eight to ten yards behind the tackle and look for the primary receiver (flanker). If the defensive back follows the curl, the tight end should be open on his swing and up. The third receiver on that side is the tailback who was added with the letter "A." The split end is used basically as a decoy in this pattern.

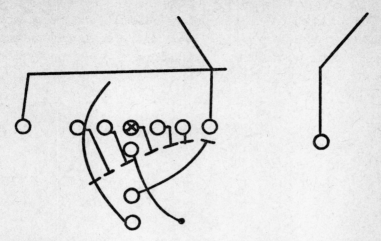

Diagram 11–2

Roll 3-C

The split end on the roll 3-C coming under would probably be the main receiver, with the tailback delaying and going behind him as the secondary receiver. The same rules apply for the line, fullback, and quarterback. If a long pass is desired, the tailback's pattern is eliminated, and he will block wherever needed.

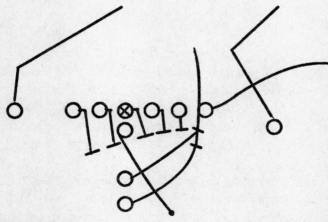

Diagram 11–3

Roll 2-B

On the roll 2-B, a quick pattern to the tight end if open would cause the quarterback to set up more quickly. If the tight end is not open, the flanker on the flag or tailback on delay seam inside would be the necessary receivers.

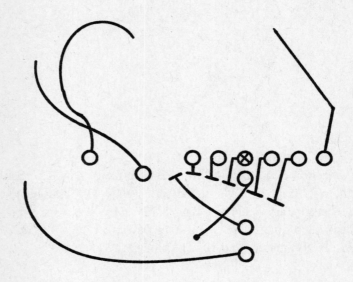

Diagram 11-4   **Roll 6-A**

The roll 6-A puts both speed receivers on the same side with the curl as the main pattern. As in the 4 pattern, pressure is put on the defensive back.

The tailback in the flare is a safety valve. The line and fullback will not use roll left blocking because of the number indicated in the pattern.

All hook patterns with the tailback flaring to the weakside may open the hook area for the tight end on the roll 9-D. The inside middle hook zone is used by the middle receiver, in this case the flanker.

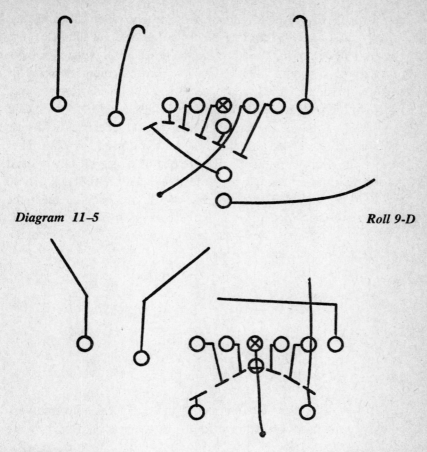

Diagram 11–5 **Roll 9-D**

Diagram 11–6 **Dropback 7-C**

The fullback will always block toward the call on the dropback series. The center is the pivot man on this protection. The "C" call will release the tailback on delay seam behind the tight end drag pattern.

QUICKS

There are two types of quick patterns in the Pro-I—one with a fake and one without. The fake will be a dive to hold the linebacker and open the inside pass routes for the receivers. In all cases, the word "quick" means a chop block to be used by the line. The players will fire out at the knees of the defender playing over them making the defenders bend down to protect themselves. This will give the quarterback a chance to see over the defensive line. Blocking the linebacker has already been discussed *(Diagrams 9–2 & 9–4)* and will be the same for the quicks. The backfield pass patterns will be called, blocking patterns followed, or play fakes carried out. The quarterback will take one quick step backward and deliver the ball immediately after the dive fake. The fullback will do most of the faking. The quarterback will step back to meet the fullback and then raise up to pass the ball. Two basic patterns are used for our quick series—the look-in *(Diagram 11–7)* and the swing *(Diagram 11–8)*.

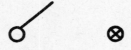

Diagram 11–7

The look-in is run at a 45° angle, and the ball is delivered very quickly. It is used when the defender is playing back and to the outside of the receiver.

Diagram 11–8

The swing is a quick type of out pattern used when the defender is playing to the inside of the receiver. The ball is thrown over the defender since the defender would be in position to knock down or intercept any pass thrown straight at the receiver. A swing and up can also be used by the receivers in this series if the defender is playing so tight that any type of short pattern is covered *(Diagram 11–9)*.

Diagram 11–9

The quarterback in this case would take his original step back, use a pump fake to make the defender commit himself more to a short area, then throw the ball in a high arch to the inside shoulder of the receiver. A second short quick step back may be used by the quarterback after the pump fake to give more room between himself and the defensive lineman. The tight end will stay in and block using the chop block unless the pass is called to him. If the original pattern is blocked off for some reason, he may also be used as a safety valve after blocking.

The backfield patterns in the quick passing series will be determined by the call in the huddle. A dive fake, either right or left, makes the fullback fake the dive and the tailback go in any direction he wishes from any formation he wants to line up in, such as with a quick dive pass right, split end look-in *(Diagram 11–10)*.

A coaching point here is to have both wide receivers run the same pattern so the quarterback knows what the other receiver is doing. The quarterback may also want to throw to the other receiver if the coverage changes on the primary target.

The backs can also get into the pass route by calling a pattern for them, such as the quick flanker look-in backs flare *(Diagram 11–11)*.

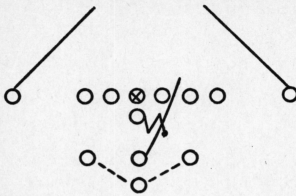

Diagram 11–10

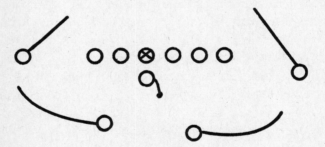

Diagram 11–11

The other main responsibility for the backs is blocking. On a swing and up to any receiver, both backs should be kept in for blocking purposes. Blocking defensive ends aggressively or helping out inside will depend on the type of defense being used by the opponent for that particular week. The quick split end swing and up is an example of such a blocking pattern *(Diagram 11–12)*. (The directions of the backs' blocks can be determined just before the play starts by verbal calls between the backs.)

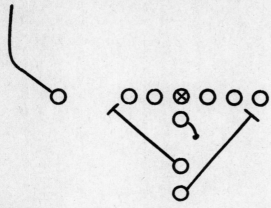

Diagram 11–12

12

EMPLOYING SCREENS AND DRAWS IN THE MULTIPLE PRO-I

The draws and screens in the Pro-I are included in the passing game because they come off a pass fake. We can draw to either back off of any backfield motion and lead the other back through the hole by adding the word "lead" (for example, lead dive) to the play. We can block the draws in many ways depending on the defense and what blocking pattern you wish to use. The screens, on the other hand, don't have as many ways to block as the draws in the Pro-I, but they can still be used effectively.

DRAWS

The fullback is the main running back used for the draws in the Pro-I. We use him because the draw is an inside running play and the fullback should be a more durable running back. It also fits in very well with the fullback going to the side of the call in the roll out series. We do not put the fullback in any specific position for the draw. He is told where we want the exchange, and it is up to him to get there. The exchange will take place about five to six yards deep and on the outside leg of the guard on the roll out draw *(Diagram 12–1)*, and behind the guard on the drop back draw *(Diagram 12–2)*.

Diagram 12–1   *Diagram 12–2*

Some of the backfield formations used for the roll out draws would be the I formation *(Diagram 12–3)*, white formation *(Diagram 12–4)*—right draws—and the I formation *(Diagram 12–5)* and white switch *(Diagram 12–6)*—left draws. (A white switch is where the tailback and fullback switch positions in a white formation.)

Diagram 12–3

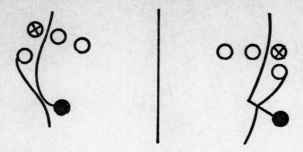

Diagram 12-4   *Diagram 12-5*

Diagram 12-6

On the drop back draw, the word "right" or "left" tells the fullback what guard to move to when expecting the ball—for example, in the drop back right draw *(Diagram 12-7)* and the drop back left draw *(Diagram 12-8)*.

Diagram 12-7

Diagram 12-8

A lead draw to either back can be run by calling the word "lead" and saying who is to carry the ball—for example, with the roll right fullback draw lead *(Diagram 12-9)*. The tailback in this play must position himself so that he can get in front of the ball carrier without interfering with the handoff or running lane. Another example of this would be the roll right tailback draw lead *(Diagram 12-10)*. On this play, we changed responsibilities of the backs. The handoff may come a little deeper because of the position of the tailback when the ball was snapped.

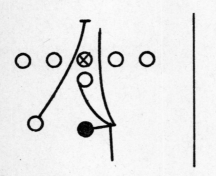

Diagram 12-9

Diagram 12-10

The blocking patterns used in the line for the draw can be the same as any inside running play. Some are more practical than others, but all could theoretically be used. An example would be the tackle trap block—not very practical, but possible if you had the personnel to run it.

We stay with a certain number of blocks with which we have enjoyed a lot of success. The diagrams that follow will be of the roll out draw and to the right. The blocking patterns can very easily be run from a drop back draw and in either direction. Drawing them this way will provide a base from which to work.

The most common block for the draw in the Pro-I is the 3 block, where every lineman blocks his own area and takes the defender in any direction he wants to go *(Diagram 12–11)*.

ΩΩ⊗ΩΩ

Diagram 12–11

The next most common block is the 2 block. On the draw, we want both sides to use the block so the running back has more area to run to. He keys the center's block *(Diagram 12–12)*. (The guards may take a drop step to show pass if the coach wishes. In the regular 2 block, the guard fires out at the tackle if he is to go first.)

Diagram 12–12

The 5 block on the side of the play is an excellent block if the center is quick enough and the linebackers are retreating quickly *(Diagram 12–13)*.

Diagram 12–13

The trapping game can also be used if that part of your game is employed often enough to inspire faith in it. The trap can be run in either direction but is usually run away from the back field flow for instance, in the roll out fullback draw right, trap left block *(Diagram 12–14)*.

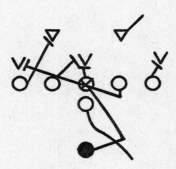

Diagram 12–14

SCREENS

The draws are blocked just like part of the running game in the Pro-I, but the screens are special. The same responsibilities hold true in the screens even down to who is in the screen itself. The tackle on the side of the roll cut will always block aggressively— just as though a pass is being thrown. The weakside tackle will retreat just like a roll out pass away. In the drop back screens, both

the tackles will retreat as they would in a pass. On the side of the
screen, the tackle's responsibility now changes. Once in position
and usually after the first hit on the rusher, the tackle will throw his
inside shoulder to the far knee of the defender. This will cause the
defender to bend down to protect his legs, thus giving the quarterback room to see his receiver *(Diagram 12–15)*.

FAR KNEE

Diagram 12–15

    Since we run most of the screen away from the flow, the
aggressive tackle and the tackle who attacks the far knee are not the
same. As the ball is snapped, both guards and the center retreat just
like a pass play is forming. The lead guard should count two seconds and then go straight down the line of scrimmage to start forming the screen. When the center sees the lead guard go, he follows
and likewise the trail guard. As they approach the area where the
receiver will make the catch, each has an assignment to carry out.
The lead guard will block the first man that appears outside. The
defender may be on the line of scrimmage or anywhere downfield.
If the lead guard's block is not needed on the line of scrimmage, he
will turn upfield *(Diagram 12–16)*. The center will be looking
downfield to block the first defender attacking the screen from the
inside *(Diagram 12–17)*. The trail guard is responsible for any defender who was not fooled and is following the receiver. If no
defender is there, he will turn upfield and look to his inside *(Diagram 12–18)*. The whole screen should look like *Diagram 12–19*.

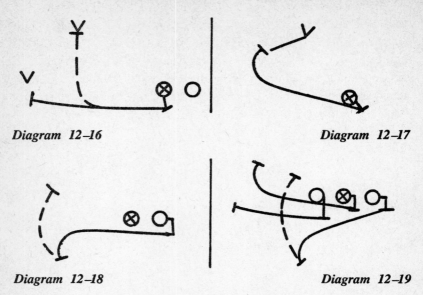

Diagram 12–16   *Diagram 12–17*

Diagram 12–18   *Diagram 12–19*

If the screen goes in the other direction, the guards will change responsibilities. The tailback will "hide" behind his offensive tackle on the side of the screen, count two seconds, and release outside to catch the pass. The pass should be caught five to seven yards deep and outside enough to get away from inside pursuit. The tailback will yell "go" when the ball is caught to let the linemen know to start upfield. A roll out right tailback screen left would look like *Diagram 12–20*.

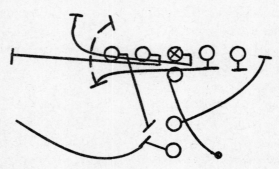

Diagram 12–20

Any number of screens can be run as far as backfield maneuvers are concerned, but the line will stay the same. A few backfield patterns with screens might be roll right, fake fullback draw, tailback screen left *(Diagram 12–21)*, or lead dive left, tailback screen right *(Diagram 12–22)*.

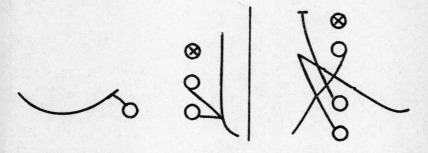

Diagram 12–21   **Diagram 12–22**

PLAY ACTION PASSES

Play action passes work only if the running plays they come from are successful. The pass can sometimes set up the run, but not very often. The action pass patterns are practiced the same as our other passes, but the faking will come only in team work on a very limited basis.

Our main action passes are called GOBs (Guard Opposite Backs). When this is called, it means pass. The GOB comes off a dive fake, but the patterns run dictate it to be a longer type pass than the dive pass from the quick series. Since all patterns have been shown (Chapter 10) and backfield patterns and any pulling guard responsibilities discussed (Chapter 9), we will draw up only play action passes. Again, for simplicity's sake, the tight end will always be right, and most plays are drawn to the right *(Diagrams 12–23 to 12–29)*.

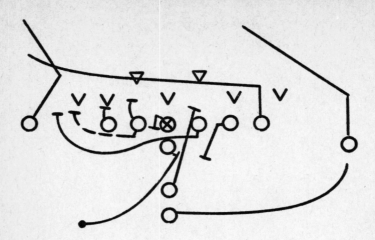

Diagram 12–23   ***GOB Right***

SE—Action flag	FB—Fill for guard/delay release
TE—Drag	behind TE
Fl—Post	TB—Flare to right

(The onside guard has a choice if the linebacker is on him. He can seal the area or pull to the outside. Other linemen will use the roll out rules.)

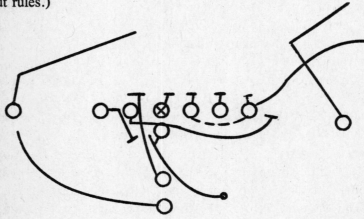

Diagram 12–24   ***GOB Left***

SE—Post   TB—Flare to left
TE—Swing   FB—Fill for guard/delay seam pattern
Fl—Action flag

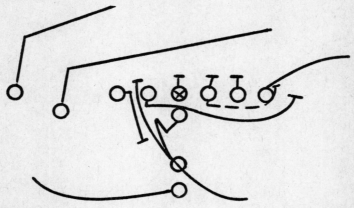

Diagram 12-25   ***Slot GOB Left***

SE—Post   TB—Flare
Fl—Deep drag   FB—Fill for guard/delay seam
TE—Swing

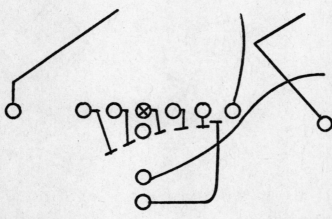

Diagram 12-26   ***Slant Pass Right***

SE—Post
TE—Fly
Fl—Action flag
FB—Swing

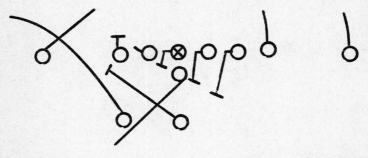

Diagram 12–27   **Slip Pass Left**

SE—Look-in
TB—Swing

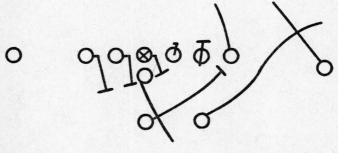

Diagram 12–28   **Slip Pass Right**

TE—Look-in
Fl—Look-in
TB—Swing

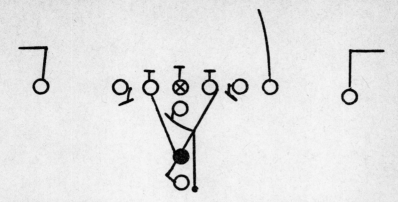

Diagram 12-29   **Counter Pass Right Tight End Fly**

Outside receivers can do any pattern as long as they stay out of the tight end's way.

13

CALLING THE PLAYS

SETTING UP THE HUDDLE

We use the open type of huddle simply because we like it better and feel better in it—and the members in the huddle can see the defense, which may help them find their blocks and running lane, or identify the type of coverage going to be used on the receivers. The center forms the huddle about ten yards from the ball. The weakside guard is on the center's left, and the weakside tackle is outside left of the guard. The strongside guard and tackle are to the right of the center, in that order. They have their hands on their knees so the players behind can see (Diagram 13–1). The second row from left to right facing the defense will consist of the split end, tailback, flanker, fullback, and tight end (Diagram 13–2). (We put our tight

end right because he will line up right most of the time.) The
complete huddle will look like *Diagram 13–3*.

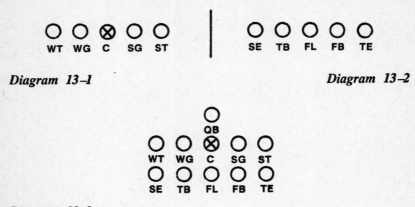

Diagram 13–1   Diagram 13–2

Diagram 13–3

    Since all plays are called from the bench, the open huddle gives
the messenger a better route to the quarterback. Over the years, we
have used four different positions to rotate plays, and the only
trouble we have had is when the player's regular huddle position is
in the back row. We then let him stay in the front of the huddle off to
one side *(Diagram 13–4)*. The quarterback will stand two yards in
front of the first line and will repeat the play twice, once to his right
and once to his left. The center and wide receivers may leave after
the first call if desired. We release the center and wide receivers
ourselves so we can get set on the ball more quickly and run on the
first sound without slowing down the natural rhythm or leaving the
linemen in their stance too long. We break the huddle with the
quarterback saying "Ready . . . break." On the word "break," the
team members will also say "break," clap their hands at the same
time, and approach the line of scrimmage. The linemen will immediately place their hands on the ground so they can fire out with
authority if the snap comes on the first sound.

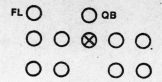

Diagram 13-4

CALLING OFFENSIVE PLAYS

Since we use a descriptive play calling system, we feel the team will have no problem adjusting to any play we call. All running plays are descriptive, as discussed in Chapter 5. Passes are called rollout or dropback, with numbered patterns. Any play action pass will have the word "pass," "GOB," or "quick" (Chapter 11), and the blocking patterns are numbered as discussed in Chapter 4. No two numbered areas will be used at the same time. For example, the passing pattern numbers will never be used in the same play with a blocking pattern number. By doing this, we feel that we can and do keep our passing and running game language separate in the huddle.

The play is called in the following sequence: formation, play, blocking pattern, and finally, snap count. The last three will always be called in that order, but the formation may or may not be called due to a variety of reasons. If the coach wants the team in a particular formation, he will call it. If the play can be run from any formation, the formation call may be omitted and certain people can line up wherever they want. In addition, certain plays must be run from the specific formations and through the week of practice can be drilled or called as part of the huddle. For example, when the fullback is to run the ball over the guard on the right side, it can be stated as follows:

Brown, fullback dive right, 3 block, first hut *(Diagram 13-5)*

I, fullback dive right, 3 block, first hut *(Diagram 13-6)*

or just

Fullback dive right, 3 block, first hut *(Diagram 13–7)*

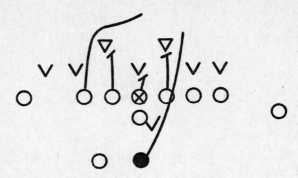

Diagram 13–5

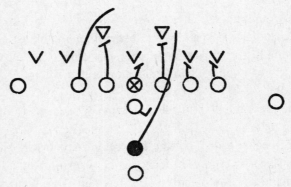

Diagram 13–6

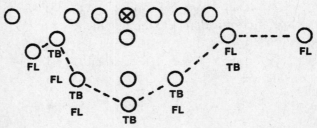

Diagram 13–7

The first two give specific formations so the team will line up that way and run the play. The third call can now release the tailback and the flanker to line up anywhere they want. By doing this, the defense cannot key on the play called. The only danger would be in making sure neither lines up at the same place every time a certain play is called, or a key will develop unconsciously. *Diagram 13–7* gives some of the different positions the tailback and flanker could use.

Some examples of other plays that could be called are:

Roll 4, First Sound. (Diagram 13–8). First sound means that on the first word that comes out of the quarterback's mouth, the ball will be snapped. No blocking calls at the line of scrimmage are made, and the quarterback must wait until everyone is set before making his sound.

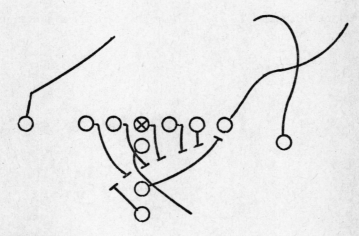

Diagram 13–8

Slant Left, 3 Block, First Hut. (Diagram 13–9). This play must be run from the I formation, and no formation call is needed.

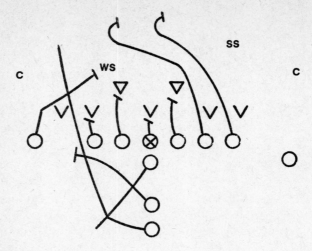

Diagram 13–9

GOB Right, First Hut. (Diagram 13–10). Formation and patterns are both previously set.

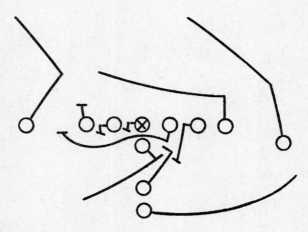

Diagram 13–10

Gold, Fullback Dive Left, 3 Block, First Hut. (Diagram 13–11). We want the tailback to line up and possibly go away from the hole area in case the defense is keying him on this play.

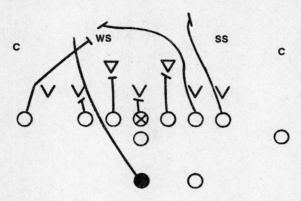

Diagram 13–11

Tackle Trap Right, First Hut. (Diagram 13–12). Formation, play and block are all stated in the play.

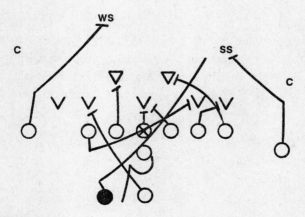

Diagram 13–12

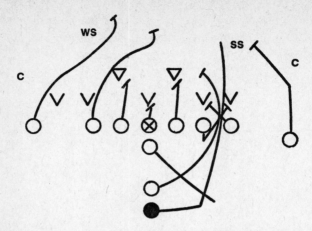

Diagram 13–13   **Tailback Slant Right, 0 Block, First Hut**

WT—Running lane
WG—BAS
 C—BAS
SG—BAS
ST—0 block rule
TE—0 block rule
FB—0 block rule

Some examples of how one play can be blocked in different ways are the slant and counter. For simplicity, we will draw up only those for the right. We have four ways to block the slant. In each case the play will be called the same way except for the blocking patterns.

WT—Running lane   ST—1 block rule
WG—BAS   TE—1 block rule
 C—BAS   FB—1 block rule
SG—1 block rule

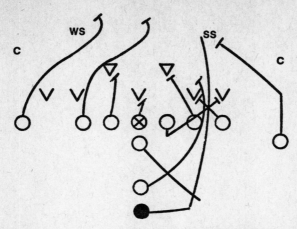

Diagram 13–14   **Tailback Slant Right, 1 Block, First Hut**

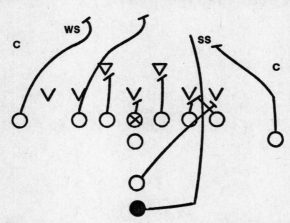

Diagram 13–15   **Tailback Slant Right, 2 Block, First Hut**

WT—Running lane   TE—22 block rule
WG—BAS   FB—22 block rule, J-block
  C—BAS
SG—BAS
ST—22 block rule

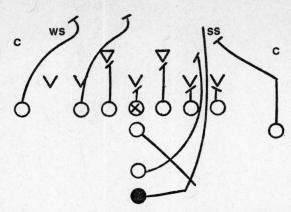

Diagram 13–16   **Tailback Slant Right, 3 Block, First Hut**

WT—Running lane   ST—3 block rule
WG—BAS   TE—3 block rule
 C—BAS   FB—3 block rule
SG—3 block rule

The tailback counter right can be blocked three ways for sure; it can be blocked two other ways (the 5 block and the tackle trap) if the right personnel are available.

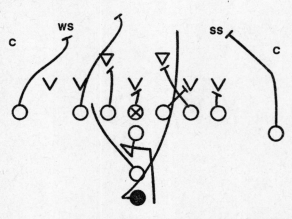

Diagram 13–17   **Tailback Counter Right, 2 Block, First Hut**

WT—Running lane   ST—2 block
WG—BAS   TE—BAS
  C—BAS   FB—Fake dive
SG—2 block   All—BAS

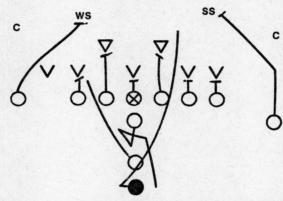

Diagram 13–18   ***Tailback Counter Right, 3 Block, First Hut***

All—BAS

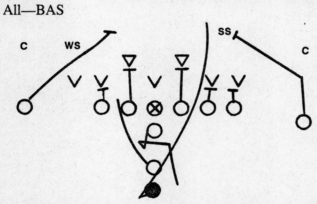

Diagram 13–19 *Tailback Counter Right, Trap Right Block, First Hut*

Line—use trap right blocking
FB—Fake dive

With other running plays in the Pro-I offense, the tailback and flanker are not drawn on, which means they can line up any place they want as long as they can only stay out of the ball carrier's way or the blocking patterns. For example, see *Diagram 13–20*.

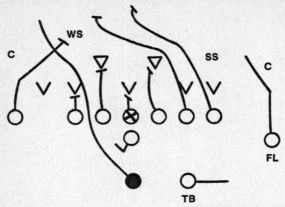

Diagram 13–20   **Fullback Dive Left, 3 Block**

SE—Running lane	SG—BAS
WT—BAS	ST—Running lane
WG—BAS	TE—Running lane
C—BAS	

Tailback Lead Dive Right 3 Block. (Diagram 13–21). The

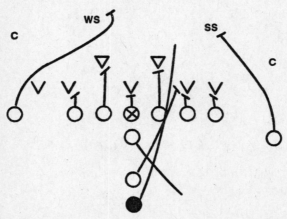

Diagram 13–21   All—BAS rules

word lead here means the fullback will lead the ta lback through the hole and block the first off color jersey. This pla is good for short yardage.

    Tailback Counter Left, 2 Block. (Diagram 13–22). The counter left, like the counter right, can be blocked three ways for sure, with two additional possible blocks, depending on personnel.

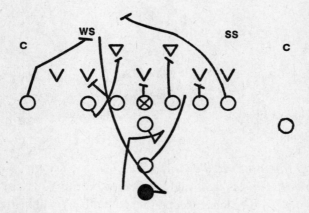

Diagram 13–22

WT—2 block	SG—BAS
WG—2 block	ST—BAS
C—BAS	TE—Running lane

    Slip Left, 3 Block (Weakside). (Diagram 13–23). The blocking patterns here are limited by the loss of a blocker (the tight end). Usually only one blocking pattern is good on this play to the weakside.

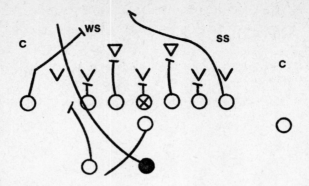

Diagram 13-23

FB—J-block	SG—BAS
WT—3 block	ST—BAS
WG—3 block	TE—Running lane
C—BAS	

Slip Right Strongside (Diagram 13-24). This area now has an extra blocker in the tight end. Different blocking patterns may be used similar to the slant, except now the tailback will be the blocker and the fullback will carry the ball. The slip right will always be run from a gold formation.

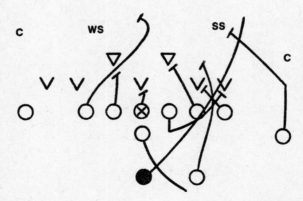

Diagram 13-24   *Gold, Slip Right, 1 Block*

WT—Running lane   ST—1 block rule

WG—BAS   TE—1 block rule

  C—BAS   TB—1 block rule

SG—1 block rule

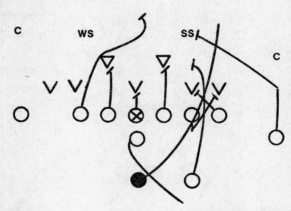

Diagram 13–25   **Gold, Slip Right, 0 Block**

WT—Running lane   ST—0 block rule

WG—Running lane   TE—0 block rule

  C—BAS   TB—0 block rule

SG—BAS

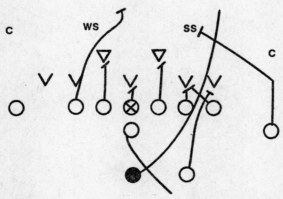

Diagram 13–26   **Gold, Slip Right, 22 Block**

WT—Running lane   ST—22 block rule
WG—Running lane   TE—22 block rule
   C—BAS   TB—22 block rule, J-block
SG—BAS

Tackle Traps. The tackle traps must also be run from a formation which enables the fullback to fill for the pulling tackle. The two plays in *Diagrams 13–27 & 13–28* are examples.

In both plays the tackle trap rules for the lineman will be used (Chapter 6). By separating the blocking patterns from the running routes, many different combinations can be used without changing assignments.

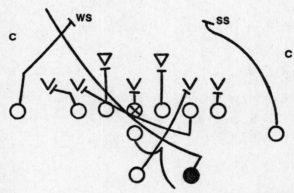

Diagram 13–27   *Tackle Trap Left*

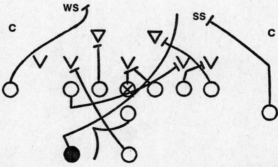

Diagram 13–28   *Tackle Trap Right*

AUDIBLES

Our audible system is a very simple one which goes well with the regular system. We do put numbers on our audibles but limit our play selection greatly. We cannot change every play in our regular system into an audible, but then we feel we shouldn't have to. We have our audibles broken down as follows: tailback sweeps, fullback dives, quicks, and slip passes. If the need arises where a stunting defense can be trapped, we add the traps. We give each play area a number sequence, and whatever number is called is what play is called. For example, any second digit number from one to four means the running play is going right. From six to nine means the play will go left. The first digit will give the play, tens for sweeps and twenties for dives. Therefore, a play called at the line of scrimmage as "12" would be a tailback sweep right, as would a call of "14." A tailback sweep left would be "19"; a fullback dive right would be "22"; and a fullback dive left would be "27."

The passes are a little different in the Pro-I audible system. The sequence consists of nineties, with ninety-one to ninety-four being swing patterns for all receivers and ninety-six to ninety-nine being looking patterns for all receivers. The key for the slip pass is "95," and the direction called is denoted by adding the letter "R" or "L." For example "95-L" is a slip pass left, while "95-R" is a slip pass right.

The key used to set the audible in motion is a color called before the number. Every week a different color can be designated as the "live" color. Other colors would be "dummy" colors. For example, if brown was the live color for the week and the quarterback called brown 14, the play would be changed from what was called in the huddle to a tailback sweep right. If the call by the quarterback was green 14, the play called in the huddle would be run because green is a "dummy" color.

We feel that these are all the audibles needed, since our blocking can usually handle any type of defense. The audibles are reserved simply for a situation where an offensive play is called and the defense outnumbers us in that area.

14

PRO-I VS. 5-2

Two of the most common defenses used by high schools throughout the nation today are the 5-2 (Fifty, Fist, 304) and the Split 6 (4-4). In order to prepare ahead of time for these defenses, certain rules have been established which should enable the offense to run without obstruction. Chapters 14 and 15 show how the Multiple Pro-I offense is diagrammed against these two defenses. The blocking rules and offensive patterns given will allow the offense to run any of the plays in previous chapters with success.

When encountering the dive, for instance:

Coaching Points (Diagram 14–1) The center and the tackle must try to turn the defender away from the hole. The block on the far backer must anticipate linebacker movement toward the play. The guard's block may be a ride type across the hole, a turn block at the point of contact, or a chop block. The on-side guard's block will be optional. The guard will take the linebacker in any direction he can, with the ball carrier blocking off the head of the blocker. The pattern for all running lane blocks are as close behind the linebacker as possible to the hole and square up to block downfield.

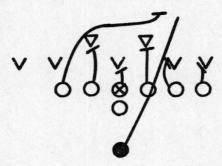

Diagram 14–1   *FB Dive Right 3 Block*

WT—Running lane   ST—2 block
WG—BAS   TE—BAS or running lane
C—BAS
SG

Coaching Points: (Diagram 14–2) The cross block at the hole will help set up the guard's angle to block the defensive tackle. The defensive tackle then attacks the linebacker with the same technique the guard uses. All other blocks are the same as discussed in *Diagram 14–1*. The dive run with the 2 block will give the defense a different blocking pattern to look at. Also, the offense can take advantage of quick offensive linemen.

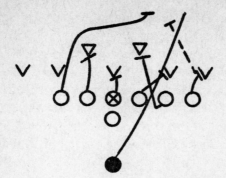

Diagram 14-2   **FB Dive Right 2 Block**

WT—Running lane   SG
WG—RAS   ST—3 block
  C—BAS   TE

Coaching Points: (Diagram 14-3) Play will help with the weakside attack when the defensive tackle is playing nose on the

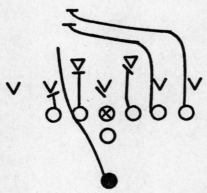

Diagram 14-3   **FB Dive Left 3 Block**

WT—3 block   SG—BAS
WG   ST—Running lane
  C—BAS   TE

offensive tackle. The same basic principles are applied with the tackle, center, and both guards.

Coaching Points: (Diagrams 14–4 a, b and c) The play is to the weak side with a different blocking pattern. The play is drawn up with the defensive tackle nose on with the offensive tackle, but it is better if the defensive tackle moves into the gap between the offensive tackle and the guard. The offensive tackle then must attack the linebacker by either going around or behind the defensive tackle.

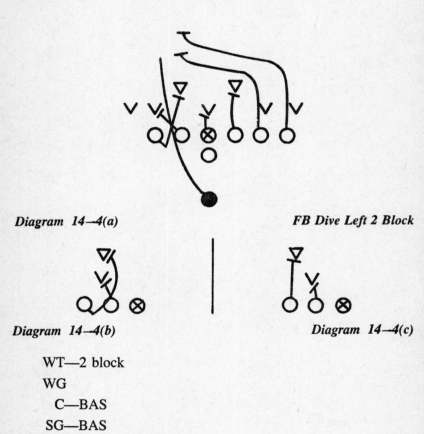

Diagram 14—4(a)   **FB Dive Left 2 Block**

Diagram 14—4(b)   *Diagram 14—4(c)*

WT—2 block
WG
  C—BAS
SG—BAS
ST—Running lane
TE

COUNTERS VS. 5-2

WT—Cut off DT; running lane.   ST—2 block

WG—BAS   ST

C—BAS   TE—BAS

Coaching Points: (Diagram 14–5 & 14–6) Being the sister play of the dive, the counter is used to take advantage of fast pursuing linebackers. The center's block is also helped by the initial move of the backs. The angle of the block by the guard will help cut down any pursuit angle of the defensive tackle. The offensive tackle block on the linebacker will be helped if the linebacker is going with the first movement in the backfield.

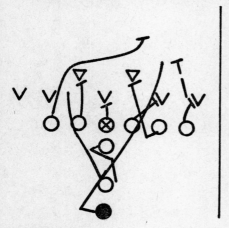

Diagram 14–5

TB Counter Right 2 Block

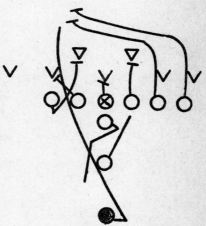

Diagram 14–6

TB Counter Left 2 Block

WT—2 block   TE—Lane

WG—2 block

C—BAS

SG—BAS

ST—Running

WT—BAS   ST—SUBA
WG—Trap   TE—BIB
  C—BAS   FB—Fill for trapping guard
SG—Lead

Coaching Points: (Diagrams 14–7 & 14–8) Trap blocking gives the defense another blocking pattern to worry about. If the defense has a good nose guard, the double team will help cut down the effectiveness. If the linebacker on the side of the hole hesitates at all, the BIB block of the end will clear him out of the hole. This play can also be added to your trapping game if you have personnel available.

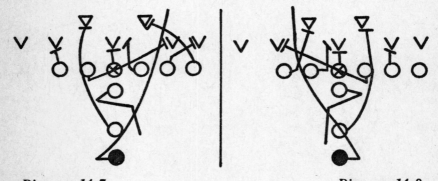

Diagram 14–7   *Diagram 14–8*

TB Counter Right Trap Block   **TB Counter Left Trap Block**

WT—BIB
WG—Lead
  C—BAS
SG—Trap
ST—BAS
TE—Running lane
FB—Fill for trapping guard

Coaching Points: (Diagram 14–9) The slant could be the number one play for your tailback. The 1 block gives a short trap at the hole and a fullback and pulling guard to add more power. The toughest block on this play is the outside tackle block on the linebacker. This is why the fullback and guard are both to look inside once they reach the hole. The off-side guard pulling will be an option depending upon your personnel. If the guard cannot pull, he will attack the linebacker in front of him. If he pulls, his first job is to clean up any penetrating defenders and pull up at the point of attack.

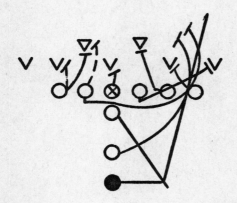

Diagram 14–9   ***TB Slant Right 1 Block***

WT—BAS—Running lane or cut off LB

WG—BAS or pull through hold looking inside

  C—BAS

SG—1 block

ST—1 block

TE—1 block

FB—Lead through hole looking inside

Coaching Points: (Diagram 14–10) The 0 block will offer a better chance to block the linebacker with the guard. The fullback is also assigned inside to help with the linebacker. The pulling off-side guard is still optional.

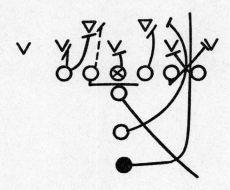

Diagram 14–10   **TB Slant Right 0 Block**

WT—Same option   ST—0 block
WG—Same option   TE—0 block
C—BAS   FB—Same
SG—BAS

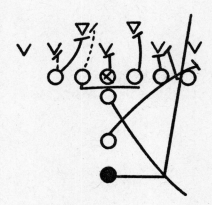

Diagram 14–11   **TB Slant Right 22 Block**

WT—Same option	ST—Double team
WG—Same option	TE—double team
C—BAS	FB—J-block
SG—BAS	

Coaching Points: (Diagram 14–11) The double team will help neutralize a big defensive tackle. The fullback block should be a good J pattern. Using this block takes away one blocker going through the hole.

Coaching Point: (Diagrams 14–12 a, b and c) Play should be run to help with the weakside running game. If the defensive tackle is in the gap and the linebacker is stacked, the two combos can be used. The pattern to be used will depend on the offensive line personnel.

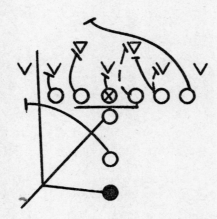

Diagram 14–12(a)   **TB Slant Left 3 Block**

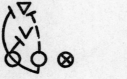   

Diagram 14–12(b)   **Diagram 14–12(c)**

WT—BAS TE—Running lane
WG—BAS FB—J-block
 C—BAS
SG—Pull through hole or BAS
ST—Cut off LE or BAS

SLIPS VS. 5-2

Coaching Points—for All Slip Rights: (Diagrams 14–13, 14–14 & 14–15)) The different blocking patterns used are to give the defense something to look at. The blocking pattern used will be determined by your offensive personnel, defensive personnel, or defensive formations.

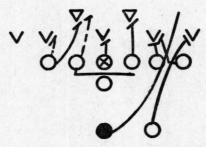

Diagram 14–13   **FB Slip Right 22 Block**

WT—Cut off LB or running lane
WG—Pull through hole on BAS
 C—BAS
SG—BAS
ST—22 block
TE—22 block
TB—J-block

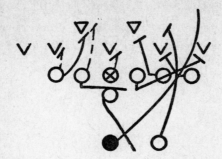

Diagram 14–14　　　　　　　　　　　**FB Slip Right 1 Block**

WT—Cut off LB or running lane　　ST—1 block
WG—Pull or BAS　　　　　　　　　TE—1 block
　C—BAS　　　　　　　　　　　　TB—Load through hold
SG—1 block　　　　　　　　　　　　　looking inside

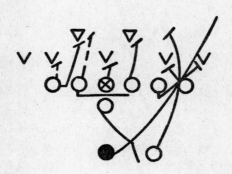

Diagram 14–15　　　　　　　　　　　**FB Slip Right 0 Block**

WT—Cut off LB or running lane　　ST—0 block
WG—Pull or BAS　　　　　　　　　TE—0 block
　C—BAS　　　　　　　　　　　　TB—Lead through hole
SG—BAS　　　　　　　　　　　　　　looking inside

Coaching Points: (Diagram 14–16) The slip should be one of your bread and butter plays to the weak side. The blocking pattern rules will be the same as the slant if the defensive tackle and linebacker stack.

WT—BAS	ST—Cut off LB or running
WG—BAS	lane
C—BAS	TE—Running lane
SG—Pull through hole or BAS	TB—J-block

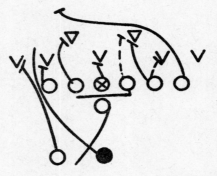

Diagram 14–16   *FB Slip Left 3 Block*

Coaching Points: (Diagrams 14–17 & 14–18) The need for a good inside running game without straight ahead blocking is essential for any offense. The blocking patterns used can attack any defender in the trap area with an angle block or a double team. Again, the type of pattern will depend on personnel.

WT—Pull, cut LB
WG—Trap
  C—MOMA
SG—Lead
ST—SUBA
TB—BIB

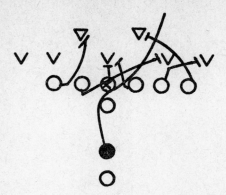

Diagram 14–17   ***FB Trap Right***

     WT—Pull, cut LB
     WG—Trap
       C—MOMA
     SG—Lead
     ST—BIB
     TE—BAS

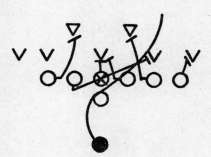

Diagram 14–18   ***FB Trap Right Switch***

   Coaching Points: (Diagram 14–19) This play is excellent to run against a good LB because of the double team.

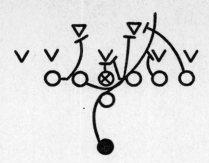

Diagram 14–19   **FB Trap Right Fold**

WT—Pull, cut LB   SG—Lead
WG—Trap on opposite LB   ST—BAS
C—MOMA   TE—BIB

TACKLE TRAPS VS. 5-2

Coaching Points: (Diagrams 14–20 thru 14–23) The tackle traps are a sister play to the slip. The tackle trapping gives a different look to the defense. The play also takes a little longer to develop, which can take advantage of fast pursuing linebackers.

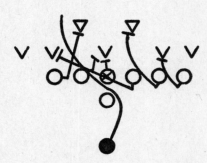

Diagram 14–20   **FB Trap Left**

WT—BIB   ST—Pull, cut LB
WG—Lead   TE—Cut DT
  C—MOMA
SG—Trap

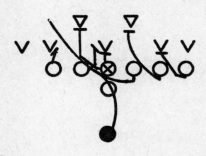

Diagram 14–21   ***FB Trap Left Fold***

WT—BAS   SG—Trap on opposite LB
WG—Lead   ST—Cut off LB
  C—MOMA   TE—Cut off DT

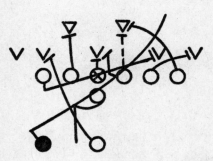

Diagram 14–22   ***Tackle Trap Right***

WT—SUBA/BIB   ST—Trap
WG—BAS/Lead   TE—Running lane
  C—BAS   FB—Fill for pulling guard
SG—BAS

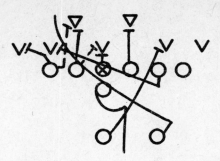

Diagram 14–23   **Tackle Trap Left**

> WT—Trap
> WG—BAS
>   C—BAS
> SG—Lead or BAS
> ST—SUBA
> TE—BIB
> FB—Fill for pulling guard

SWEEPS VS. 5-2

Coaching Points: (Diagrams 14–24 thru 14–27) The idea of
having two ways of blocking the sweep is to be able to take advantage of your offensive personnel or a weakening in the defense. The
main key is how the defensive end is playing. If he is penetrating
into the backfield, the regular block would be better because the
tight end is there to cut down the penetration. If the DE floats, the
crack back is the best block. A switch can also be called on the
crackback so the fullback will block the defensive end and the wide
receiver the strong safety.

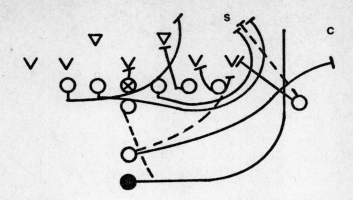

Diagram 14-24   **TB Sweep Right– Crack Back**

WT—Pull and turn up first hole past center

WG—Pull around corner, look inside

 C—BAS

SG—Pull around corner, look inside

ST—1st man inside

SE—1st man inside

FB—1st man to show outside

Fl—Crack back on DE

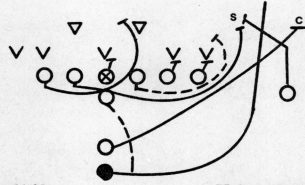

Diagram 14-25   **TB Sweep Right Regular**

WT—Same

WG—Same

 C—BAS

SG—Block LB either by attacking or pulling and blocking
   back

ST—BAS

TE—BAS

FB—1st man outside

Fl—Inside safety

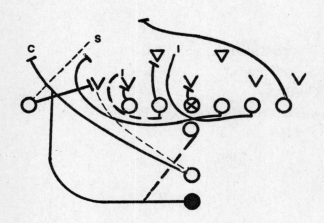

Diagram 14-26   ***TB Sweep Left Crackback***

WT—BAS

WG—Block LB either by attacking or pulling and blocki
   back

 C—BAS

SG—Pull around corner; look inside

ST—Pull and turn up first hole past center

TE—Running lane

SE—Crackback on DE

FB—1st man outside

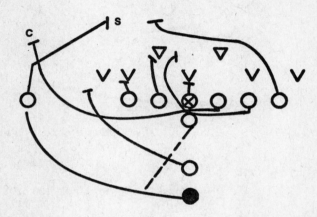

Diagram 14-27
                                                    TB Sweep Left– Regular

WT—BAS

WG—Same

  C—BAS

SG—Pull around corner block 1st man outside

ST—Same

TE—Running lane

SE—Block inside safety

FB—Block DE

Coaching Points: (Diagram 14–28) The fullback must make the play look like a dive helping the block of the strong tackle. The outside release of the tight end could cause a seam to develop inside of the defensive end. For the quarterback to keep the ball, the tailback must keep a good pitch distance from the quarterback.

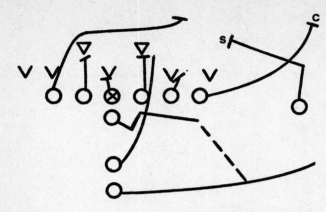

Diagram 14-28   ***Dive Option Right 3 Option Block***

WT—Running lane   ST—BAS
WG—BAS   TE—Outside release; block 1st man outside
SG—BAS   FB—Dive fake
 C—BAS   Fl—Inside safety

Coaching Points: (Diagrams 14-29a & b) The other blocks mentioned here would help on a reading defense.

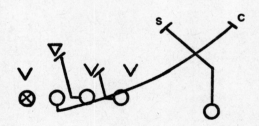

Diagram 14-29a   ***1 Option Block***

C—BAS
SG—Pull like sweep 1st man outside

ST—1 block

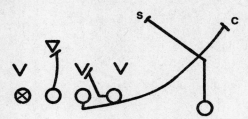

Diagram 14–29b   **0 Option Block**

TE—1 block
ST—Pull and block corner
TE—0 block

QB OPTION VS. 5-2

Coaching Points: (Diagram 14–30) This play gives an extra blocker to lead play outside.

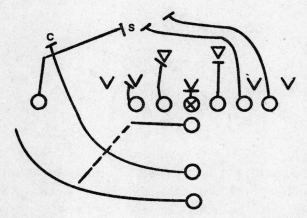

Diagram 14–30   **QB Option Left**

WT—BAS
WG—BAS
 C—BAS
SG—BAS
ST—Running lane
SE—Inside safety
FB—Post man outside

   QB option can use the following blocks: 1 option, 22, 0 option, 3 option *(Diagram 14–31)*.

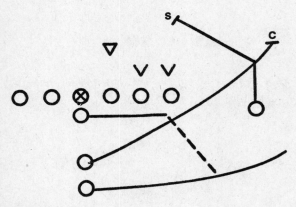

Diagram 14–31

   Coaching Points: (Diagram 14–32, 14–33 & 14–34). This play can take advantage of a good fullback. The fake straight ahead should hold the linebacker and allow any block called at the hole time to develop. The tailback can also help this play by making it look like a sweep as much as possible.

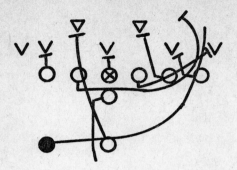

Diagram 14–32   **TB Cross Right 1 Block**

WT—BAS

WG—Pull through hole, look inside

  C—BAS

SG—1 block

ST—1 block

TE—1 block

FB—Full for pulling guard

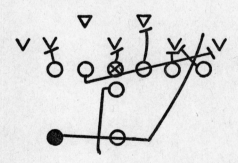

Diagram 14–33   **TB Cross Right 22 Block**

WT—BAS

WG—Pull and trap out first man outside the double team

  C—BAS

SG—BAS

ST—Double team

TE—Double team

FB—Fill for pulling guard

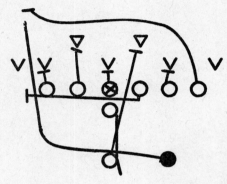

Diagram 14-34   **TB Cross Left 3 Block**

WT—BAS

WG—BAS

  C—BAS

SG—Pull and trap first man outside WT

ST—BAS

TE—Running lane

FB—Fill for pulling guard

15

ATTACKING THE SPLIT-6
WITH THE MULTIPLE PRO-I

The Split-6 defense offers a challenge to any offense because of the different look it gives. The middle of the Split-6 defense is arranged in a way that eliminates common blocking rules being used. Thus, the blocking angles will be slightly different but the basic rules for the blocking patterns can still be used effectively. Special blocking patterns will be included in Chapter 15 to take advantage of the ability and agility of your offensive linemen. The combo block, for instance, affects the guards on the play side and the center. Using the inside shoulder, the offensive guard will block the defensive tackle long enough for the offensive center to step to his side and help block the tackle. The guard then slides to the outside to block the inside linebacker.

By using the rules set forth in this chapter, then, the offense should be able to take advantage of the Split-6 for additional scoring power.

Coaching Point: When running against this defense, the fullback should stay inside until just before he hits the line of scrimmage. This will help the blocks on the defensive tackle and inside linebacker. The guard can also use the set up step to help get a good blocking angle on the defensive tackle. The strong tackle can also help dive on his side by making contact with the defensive tackle before sliding to the linebacker *(Diagram 15–1)*.

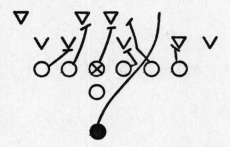

Diagram 15–1   **FB Dive Right 3 Block**

    WT—BAS (most dangerous man)

    WG—BAS

      C—BAS (on backer)

    SG—BAS

    ST—BAS (make contact with DT and slide to LB)

    TE—BAS

Coaching Point: The dive has to hit very quick because of the difficult blocking angle of the center. The center must stay with the linebacker long enough to have the running back pass him *(Diagram 15–2)*.

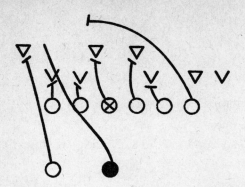

Diagram 15–2   **FB Dive Left 3 Block**

WT—BAS

WG—BAS

C—BAS

SG—BAS

ST—BAS

TE—Running lane

TB—Must attack outside LB to get LB thinking outside

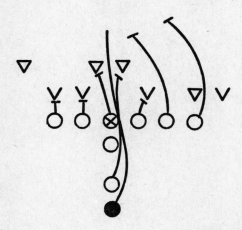

Diagram 15–3   **TB Lead Dive Right**

WT—BAS

WG—BAS

  C—BAS (weak backer)

SG—BAS

ST—Running lane

TE—running lane

FB—Lead through hole and block inside linebacker

Coaching Points: Lead dives will take advantage of blocking angle the outside guards have on the defensive tackle. The center will block the linebacker away from the hole and the fullback must block the linebacker on the side of the call. The tailbacks after receiving the ball should go straight over the center. The quarterback should get the ball back to the tailback as quickly and as deep as possible *(Diagram 15-3 & 15-4)*.

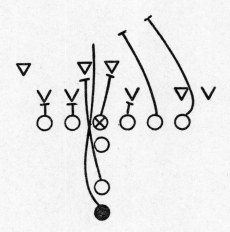

Diagram 15-4   *TB Lead Dive Left*

WT—BAS

WG—BAS

C—BAS (weak backer)

SG—BAS

ST—Running lane

TE—running lane

FB—Lead through hole and block inside backer
    (Diagram 15–4)

TB COUNTER LEFT INSIDE

This counter is very similar to the dive except that the center and fullback trade linebackers. Also, the tailback's route is a little altered in that the counter is run up the middle instead of over the guard.

Coaching Points: The inside counters are blocked just like the lead dives except for the center and the fullback exchanging blocks. The counter action taking place in the backfield will help with the angles on the linebackers *(Diagrams 15–5a & b)*.

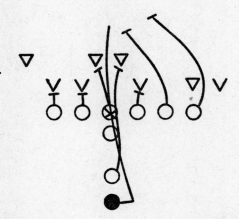

Diagram 15–5a   *Counter Vs. Split-6*

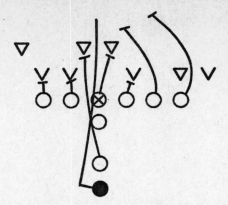

Diagram 15–5b   **TB Counter Right Inside**

Coaching Points: The regular counter is run a little wider than normal. The tailback's path is the same until the tailback almost reaches the hole. He then slides to the outside to take advantage of the blocking pattern *(Diagram 15–6)*.

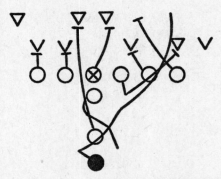

Diagram 15–6   **TB Counter Right 1 Block**

WT—Brush

WG—BAS

C—On-side backer

SG—1 block

ST—1 block

TE—1 block

FB—Fake and block backside backer

This is the regular counter where the TB will head to his guard but slide outside because of the blocking pattern. Counter to the weak side will be difficult to run because the offense is outnumbered.

SLANT VS. SPLIT-6

Coaching Point: By mixing up the pattern, the keys will be broken down for the inside backers. Slants should still be a strong running play. The blocking pattern used can be alternated to give the defense a different look. The 1 block will have a pulling guard from the weak side to help clean up in the hole. The 0 block has the good inside out angle on the defensive end, but the combo block inside is very difficult. The center must be very quick to block the defensive tackle for the play to work. The fullback can also be used to block the defensive tackle or help on the linebacker *(Diagrams 15–7 and 15–8)*.

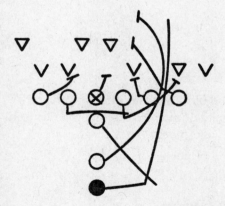

Diagram 15–7   **TB Slant Right 1 Block**

WT—BAS inside

WG—Pull or offside backer

  C—If WB pulls block offense LB; if WB blocks offside LB, block onside backer

SG—1 block

ST—1 block

TE—1 block

FB—lead through hole

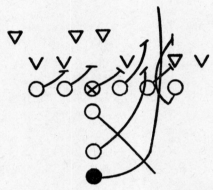

Diagram 15-8   ***TB Slant Right 0 Block***

WT—BAS

WG—Offside backer

C—Combo block—guard must stop charge of defensive tackle and slip to outside to pick up inside backer. Center must cut off DT after guard stops charge.

SG—Combo block

ST—0 block

TE—0 block

FB—Lead through hole

Coaching Points: The fullback's path will be determined by the offensive tackle's block. A dip in then out may be used to help the offensive tackle with his block. The tailback's route can also be run to catch the linebacker going to the inside *(Diagram 15–9)*.

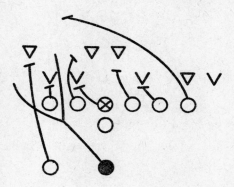

Diagram 15–9   *FB Slip Left 3 Block*

WT—BAS

WG—Combo-guard stops charge of DT then slides to outside to pick up LB. Center picks up DT after guard stops charge.

C

SG—First LB inside

ST—Cut DT

TE—Running lane

TB—Block outside LB

Coaching Points: The slip run to the tight end side can use any blocking pattern which includes the tight end. Either block can be used according to the coach's preference or need *(Diagram 15–10 & 15–11)*.

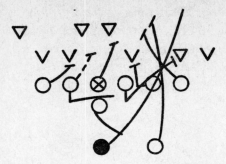

Diagram 15-10   ***FB Slip Right 1 Block***

WT—Cut DT

WG—Near backer or pull

  C—LB depending on whether guard pulls

SG—1 block

ST—1 block

TE—1 block

TB—Lead through hole

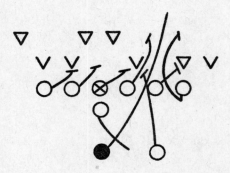

Diagram 15-11   ***FB Slip Right 0 Block***

WT—Cut DT

WG—Bear backer

    C—Combo
 SG—Combo
 ST—0 block
 TE—0 block
 TB—Lead through hole

Coaching Points: The trapping game against this defense has one block (SG) that comes across the center. His block along with the BIB block of the strong tackle is very important because of the linebacker's position. If these two blocks can be made, the trap can be run effectively. If not, the special trap can be used. The extra blocker (FB) can be used to eliminate the long BIB block of the strong guard. Also, the SUBA block on the side of the hole will slow down any fast pursuing linebackers *(Diagrams 15–12 to 15–15).*

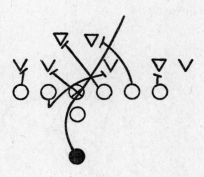

Diagram 15–12   *FB Trap Right*

    WT—BAS
 WG—Trap
    C—Man away
 SG—Far backer
 ST—BIB
 TE—BAS

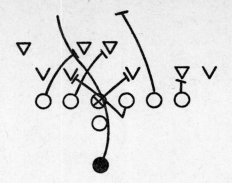

Diagram 15–13   **FB Trap Left**

WT—BIB
WG—Far backer
  C—Man away
SG—Trap
ST—Running lane
TE—BAS

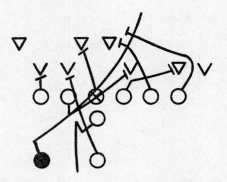

Diagram 15–14   **TB Special Trap Right**

WT—BAS
WG—Trap
  C—Off backer

SG—SUBA

ST—BIB

TE—Running lane

FB—Fill for pulling guard

TB—One false step left, then regular trap route

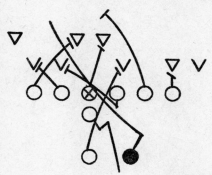

Diagram 15–15   *TB Special Trap Left*

WT—BIB

WG—SUBA

  C—Off backer

SG—Trap

ST—Running lane

TE—BAS

FB—Fill for pulling guard

TB—One false step right, then regular trap route

TACKLE TRAP VS. SPLIT-6

Coaching Points: The tackle trap is an excellent play because of the extra blocker (FB), the different trapper (T), and a delay action in the backfield. It also takes advantage of fast reacting or blitzing linebackers. The fast reacting linebackers will take themselves out of the play by going with first motion. The blitzing linebacker can be picked up by the center and the trapping tackle. The SUBA block will set up the defensive tackle for the trap and hold the linebacker if the linebacker is reading his key properly *(Diagrams 15–16 and 15–17)*.

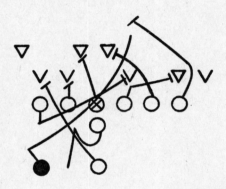

Diagram 15–16   **Tackle Trap Right**

WT—Trap   ST—BIB
WG—BAS   TE—Running lane
  C—Off backer   FB—Fill for pulling tackle
SG—SUBA

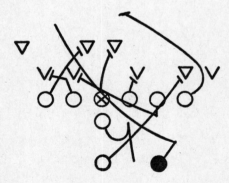

Diagram 15–17   **Tackle Trap Left**

WT—BIB	ST—Trap
WG—SUBA	TE—Running lane
C—Off backer	FB—Fill for pulling tackle
SG—BAS	

SWEEPS VS. SPLIT-6

Coaching Points: The tight end and wide receiver blocks must be made to enable the outside game to go. The pulling guards must be aware of the linebackers whether blitzing or sliding *(Diagram 15–18)*.

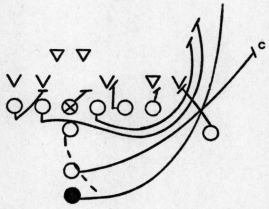

Diagram 15–18   ***TB Sweep Right***

WT—Pull, clean up

WG—Pull

  C—BAS

SG—Pull

ST—1st man inside

TE—BAS

Fl—Crackback

FG—Lead, block corner

Coaching Point: The weak tackle block must stop the penetration of the defensive end *(Diagram 15-19)*.

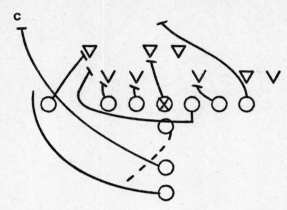

Diagram 15-19   *TB Sweep Left*

WT—BAS	ST—Pull, clean up
WG—BAS	TE—Running lane
C—BAS	SE—Crack back
SG—Pull	FB—Lead, block corner

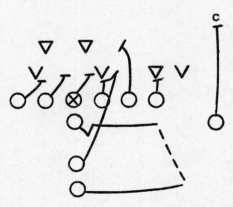

Diagram 15-20   *Dive Option Right*

WT—BAS	ST—BIB
WS—Off backer	TE—BAS
C—On backer	Fl—Corner
SG—BAS	FB—Dive fake, block DT

Coaching Point: Options should be executed on the outside defender, whether linebacker or defensive end. The fullback can help on the defensive tackle or linebacker depending on the scouting report *(Diagrams 15–20 and 15–21).*

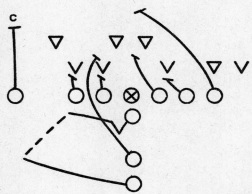

Diagram 15–21   *Dive Option Left*

WT—BAS	ST—BAS
WG—BAS	TE—Running lane
C—On backer	SE—Corner
SG—Off backer	FB—Dive fake, block on backer

Coaching Points: A good fake inside by the fullback should freeze the linebacker and help the block form at the hole. The tailback can also help the play by making it look like a sweep before squaring his route to the hole *(Diagram 15–22).*

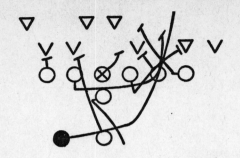

Diagram 15-22   **TB Cross Right 1 Block**

WT—BAS

WG—Pull through hole, turn in

  C—BAS

SG ⎫

ST ⎬ 1 block

TE ⎭

FB—Fill for pulling guard

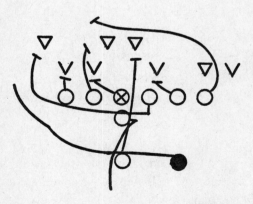

Diagram 15-23   **TB Cross Left 3 Block**

WT—BAS

WG ⎫
  C ⎭ Combo

SG—Pull, block outside LB

ST—BAS

TE—Running lane

FB—Fill for pulling guard

CROSS VS. SPLIT-6

Coaching Point: The cross to the weak side could very easily turn into a sweep, depending on the outside linebacker. If the linebacker comes across the line of scrimmage, the tailback will square to the hole. If the linebacker stays at home, the play will turn into the sweep *(Diagram 15–23).*

16

DRILLS FOR THE
MULTIPLE PRO-I OFFENSE

All drills, whenever possible, should be taught in reverse. The final position is shown first, as is each step until the stance or ready position is reached. In addition, for better use of practice time, drills for the Multiple Pro-I are broken down into three groups: the linemen, wide receivers, and running backs.

OFFENSIVE DRILLS

The main blocking drills for all positions are also broken down into three areas: contact, approach, and stance or take-off. The drills should be coached with the following points in mind:

Contact. The final position of the head is up for contact. The shoulder pad is tucked into the defender with the butt down and in, and legs apart in a good driving position. The turning, screening, and driving of the defender is then shown to get the feel of the proper position.

Approach. The head is up moving to proper positioning on the defender for the approach. The legs are apart for good balance and the weight is balanced for the impact.

Stance or Take-Off. The feet are wide enough for good balance and then should be flat (if possible), with the weight on the balls of the feet. The lineman's weight on his hands should be more than the back's but not enough to restrict movement to either side. The straight ahead block should be performed while rolling off the forward foot in the stance. a setup step to either side while blocking straight ahead can be used to help the lineman get a better blocking angle on the defender.

Purpose: To teach correct blocking procedures.

LINEMAN DRILLS

7-Man Sled *(Diagram 16–1)*

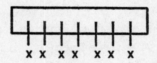

Diagram 16–1   *(One man on each pad at an arm's length away.)*

The 7-man sled is used at least three days a week for take-off, contact, and driving drills. Some of the basic drills that are used with the sled are:

1. The shot drill—Start with each lineman firing out to make contact with one shoulder without moving his feet and keep-

ing his head up. The shoulder to be used will be determined beforehand by the coach.

Purpose: To teach leg explosion and to stay down on the initial impact.

2. The shot and follow drill—The lineman will come off his stance, rolling off of his front foot and making contact with the proper shoulder while taking two steps. His tail must be down and head up in a good striking position.

Purpose: To complete the whole blocking pattern from contact to driving the defender.

Another 7-man sled drill uses just four of the seven pads while performing the drills discussed *(Diagram 16-2).* Players are aligned on every other pad. If a 7-man sled is not available or undesirable, large dummies could be used for the first two drills and a push-back dummy could be used for the third.

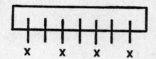

Diagram 16-2

BOARD DRILLS

Dummies are put at one end of a 2″ × 12″ × 10′ board for this drill. The blocker will drive the dummy down the board to a distance that you designate. The form used on the dummies is the same discussed earlier in the chapter.

Purpose: To review correct blocking techniques and teach the blocker to keep his feet apart.

CROSS BLOCK DRILL

The cross block drill is used for guard and tackle (2 block) or tackle end (0 block). The rule for cross blocking is free or outside man first *(Diagram 16–3)*. The blocker who blocks the down lineman must always cut off the penetration of the defender. The other blocker will drop step to clear and proceed to his area.

Purpose: To teach correct technique, positioning, and determination of who should go first on cross blocks.

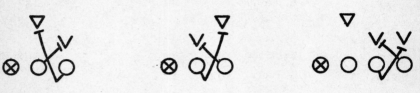

Diagram 16–3

TRAPPING DRILL

When trapping, a lineman is taught to pull the arms back while taking a jab step to square off the shoulders in the direction that he has to go. For example, if he has to pull to his right, the right elbow will be pulled back to square off his shoulders while position stepping with his right foot *(Diagram 16–4)*.

Diagram 16–4

Trapping linemen will pull down line to block one of three dummies on the trapping drill. The dummies are placed in possible defense positions. The trapper's route should always be into the line so that the trapper has good inside out position. Trapping the number one dummy will be easier because of the proper angle formed by this route. When using dummy number three, if the trapper or coach feels that it is past the danger zone, the trapper can pull through the hole and lead upfield.

Purpose: To teach the correct routes for the trapping game.

DOUBLE TEAM DRILL

The post blocker on the double team drill should use the shoulder away from the hole to stop penetration, using the rolling off of the front foot technique. The lead blocker side steps to the inside to keep the defender from splitting the double team and drives the defender straight back by being hip to hip with the post man *(Diagram 16–5)*.

Diagram 16–5

PASS BLOCKING

Pass blocking can be run two ways—man-on-man or cup. Since we do a lot of cup blocking because of our roll outs, it will be discussed first.

The cup drill should be done with an entire line. On the snap, the line will hinge upon the tackle on the side of the roll. Each lineman will step to the inside cup and turn slightly to the outside. The hinge tackle will block straight on *(Diagram 16–6)*. Any number of defensive linemen can rush, complete with stunting linebackers, on this drill. A fullback could also be added to block the end on the side of the roll. On the drop back cup, linemen will step to the inside gap (toward the center) and turn slightly to the outside. A dummy should be placed where the quarterback will set up in each drill so the linemen will know where the quarterback is supposed to be *(Diagram 16–7)*.

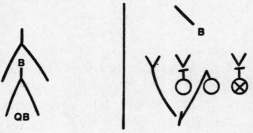

Diagram 16–6

Diagram 16–7

The man-on-man drill will require less people. The blocker will block the defender no matter where he goes, keeping in mind where the quarterback will throw from *(Diagram 16–8)*. Five-on-five can also be used to teach guards to look for the linebacker and release outside the far end *(Diagram 16–9)*.

Diagram 16–8   *Diagram 16–9*

WIDE RECEIVERS

The wide receiver has three basic blocks: the crack back on the line of scrimmage, the block back on the inside safety, and the block straight ahead on the cornerback in front of him.

Crack Back

The receiver must align himself so that he can reach the person he has to block. He cannot line up so wide that he will be late or so tight that the defender will line up on him. We tell our wide people to experiment on the defender early in the game on plays away from him or up the middle. The block must be made in a non-clip position and above the waist. The head should go on the offensive side of the defender. If the defender comes across fast, the blocker must cut off penetration. If the defender floats, the blocker can wait until the defender turns toward him. The defender in each case should be using a push-back dummy *(Diagram 16–10)*.

Purpose: To teach correct technique and positioning for the crack back blockers.

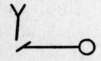   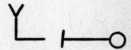

Diagram 16–10

Block on Safety

When our receiver blocks on the inside safety, we ask him to go upfield for two or three steps then go on an angle that will intercept the safety on his inside out pursuit route. The blocker should gather himself and almost "sneak up" on the defender. A push-back dummy is also used for this *(Diagram 16–11)*.

Purpose: Correct procedure for blocking inside safety man.

Diagram 16–11

Block on Corner

If the wide receiver has to block the near corner, we ask him just to put his body between the defender and the ball carrier. We call it "dancing with the defender" *(Diagram 16–12)*.

Purpose: Correct technique for blocking corner man.

Diagram 16–12

RUNNING BACKS

The running back has two basic blocks: the J-block and the lead block plus a "clean-up" type.

J-Block

On the J-block, both backs can work at the same time. The fullback will line up in his regular position, with the tailback either in the brown or gold position. On the snap called by the coach, they take a good inside out route on the defensive end so the ball carrier can break inside *(Diagram 16–13)*. After this block has been practiced, the dummy holder moves inside to simulate the defensive end reading a play inside. The blocker should then hook or turn his man to the inside so the runner can go outside. The blocker should always try for the inside out route *(Diagram 16–14)*.

Purpose: Correct positioning and technique to block the defensive end or outside linebackers.

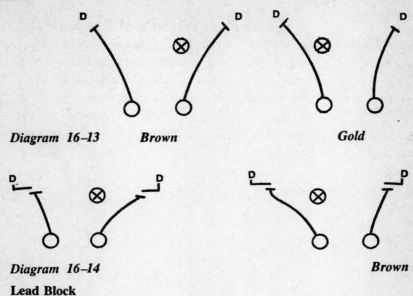

Diagram 16–13 **Brown** **Gold**

Diagram 16–14 **Brown**

Lead Block

The lead block is used when one running back blocks on an inside linebacker leading a dive play. The blocker should try to attack and destroy by smothering or turning the linebacker *(Diagram 16–15)*.

Purpose: To teach correct technique and blocking position on inside penetration.

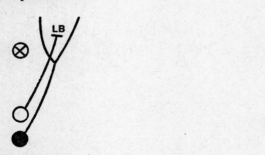

Diagram 16–15

Clean-up Block

The term clean-up block means the blocker will block the first defender that appears in the running lane. The two most common blocks of this type are the sweep block and the turn up through hole block. On the sweep block, the blocker will block the defender in the direction of movement the defender takes *(Diagram 16–16)*. A dummy holder will take the inside or outside route called by the coach and the blocker will block accordingly. The same type of block will be used on an outside linebacker to that side *(Diagram 16–17)*.

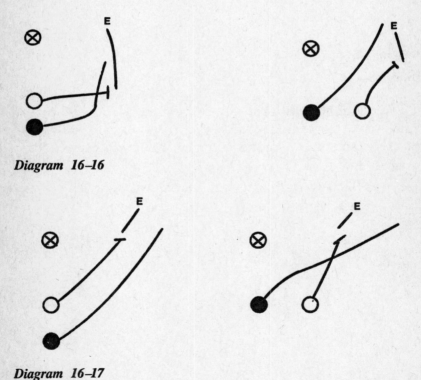

Diagram 16–16

Diagram 16–17

On the turn up block, the lead back will lead through the hole, looking to the inside of the defense. He will probably block the inside linebacker most of the time. If the linebacker does not appear, the blocker is to continue downfield and block the safety *(Diagram 16–18)*.

Purpose: To teach proper technique and positioning of the blocker's clean-up responsibility block.

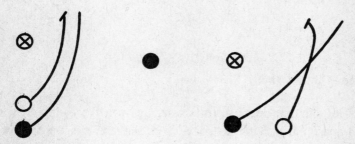

Diagram 16–18

Pass Block

In our cup pass protection, the running backs will form the outer edge of the cup. They are responsible for the outside rush man. For this drill, the backs will join the line *(Diagram 16–19)*. The fullback will always go to the right on the drop back pass. The fullback will go to the side of the roll out. The tailback will go

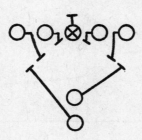

Diagram 16–19

opposite and could release for a check off pass *(Diagram 16–20).*

Purpose: Correct positioning to help pass block.

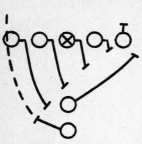 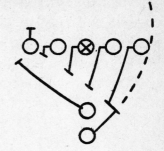

Diagram 16–20

Sideline Dummy Drill

The sideline dummy drill is set up with three dummies five yards apart and varying distances from the sideline, the first being about five yards away, the last two yards, and the middle one splitting the difference. The ball carrier will attack the dummy as if it were a tackler, using his inside arm and shoulders to protect himself and the ball. After contact is made, the ball carrier will spin to his outside with the knees high and proceed to the next dummy *(Diagram 16–21).*

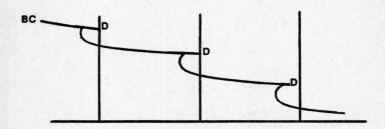

Diagram 16–21

Another ball carrier drill is the gauntlet. Four, six, eight or ten players make a small path and hit the ball carrier with push-back dummies as he tries to run between them *(Diagram 16–22)*.

Purpose: To teach the ball carrier to strike a blow to an oncoming tackle, protect the ball, and spin away from him without going out of bounds.

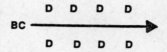

Diagram 16–22

Pass Catching Drills

In the "turn around drill," a passer and receiver stand anywhere from ten to thirty yards apart. The receiver will start with his back to the passer. The passer will then throw the ball, and when the ball gets about halfway to the receiver, the passer will yell "ball." The receiver will then jump, turn, and catch the ball.

Purpose: Used before or after practice to test the reflexes and hands of all receivers.

This drill can also be used as a bad ball drill, with the ball thrown poorly (wrong side, low, high). On the longer pass (thirty yards), the receiver will just turn the upper body to catch the ball.

Purpose: Catching balls not thrown properly.

Another pass catching drill consists of the receiver catching the ball and another player with a push-back dummy making contact with him at the same time. The force of the hit is controlled by the coach.

Purpose: Concentrating on the ball while a defender is in the area.

A passing drill using all receivers is one we have found useful because they are catching a ball on every snap. Other quarterbacks, coaches, or managers can be used to throw the balls. With five passers and five receivers, not too much time is wasted *(Diagram 16–23)*.

Purpose: To learn correct routes and catching the football on every play.

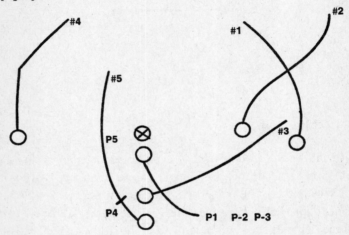

Diagram 16–23

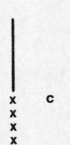

Diagram 16–24

A one handed drill may also be used. The drill may be run two different ways. In both cases, the receivers will try to catch the ball using only one hand *(Diagram 16–24)*.

Purpose: To teach the proper way to control the ball with one hand.

INDEX

Play action passes *(cont.)*
  practice, 149
  slant pass right, 151
  slip pass left, 152
  slip pass right, 152
  slot GOB left, 151
  tight end always right, 149
Plays, calling, 155-171 *(see also* Calling plays)
Positions:
  backfield, 26-27
    fullback, 26-27
    quarterback, 26
    tailback, 27
  interior linemen, 24-25
    strongside tackle, 24-25
    weakside tackle, 24
  receivers, 25-26
    split end and flanker, 25
    tight end, 25-26
Post:
  flanker, 113, 117
  split end, 103
  tight end, 109
Post Block, 18
Pulling guards, 75-76, 96-98

Q

QB option vs. 5-2, 193-196
Quarterback:
  characteristics, 27
  feet, 32
Quick passing game, 95-96
Quicks:
  backfield patterns, 137
  fake, 135
  look-in, 136
  swing, 136
  word "quick" means, 136

R

Receivers:
  feet, 31-32
  split end and flanker, 25
  stance and spacing, 30-31
  tight end, 25-26
Roll out and drop back:
  alternate responsibilities, 88-89
  area responsibility, 84-87
  blitzing linebacker, 88
Roll out draws, 142

Rolls, 131-135
Round Off, 18
Routes, trapping game, 55-56, 61-62
Royal, Darrell, 15
Running back:
  feet, 32
  stance an spacing, 30-31
Running back drills:
  ball carrier, 229
  clean-up block, 226-227
  gauntlet, 229
  J-block, 224-225
  lead block, 225
  one handed, 231
  pass block, 227-228
  pass catching, 229-231
  passing, using all receivers, 230
  sideline dummy, 228-229
  turn around, 229

S

Screen Block, 18-19
Screens, 146-149
Seam:
  fullback, 120
  tailback, 119
Seam Block, 18
Set Up Block Away, 19, 58-60
7-man sled drill:
  shot and follow, 219
  shot drill, 218-219
Shot and follow drill, 219
Shot drill, 218-219
Shoulders, 31-32
Sideline dummy drill, 228
Simplicity, 15
Slant pass right, 151
Slants, 50-53
Slant vs. Split-6, 203-209
Slip pass left, 152
Slip pass right, 152
Slips, 53-54
Slips vs. 5-2, 182-186
Slot, 20, 116
Slot GOB left, 151
Spacing, 29-32
Split end:
  characteristics, 25
  pass patterns, 100-106 *(see also* Pass patterns)
Split-6:
  cross vs., 215